"From American Dream to God's Destiny"

~⧢~

A true story of surrendering self and finding purpose.

Robert Louis Huber

XULON PRESS

From American Dream to God's Destiny
by Robert Louis Huber

Printed in the United States of America

ISBN 1-60034-475-5

Unless otherwise indicated, Bible quotations are taken from the King James Version.

www.xulonpress.com

Dedication

For Joy,
For your love, understanding and support

For Chloe, Salome,
and Jake

Acknowledgements

Mom and Dad Huber
Mom and Dad Vogt
All our siblings, grandparents, uncles, aunts and cousins
Steve Gutwein, Francesville Church
All those that pray for and support us
The Bahlers, FBi Buildings, Inc.
Jon Schwab, Industrial Pallet Corp.
AdaptaSoft Inc.
Deb Porter
John & Claudia Gross
Jerry & June Tooley
Marshall & Jan Heinold
Manuel & Gaby, Casa Elizabeth Orphanage
Casa Vida y Esperanza Orphanage
Wendell Gudeman
Mrs. Patty (Martin)
Mike Putt & Phil Gutwein
Enrique Ochoa Moreno
Rick

Foreword

⚘

He is no fool who gives up what he cannot keep,
to gain that which he cannot lose. -Jim Elliot

If there is anything I've learned so far in life, it is that I still have a lot to learn--and much of what I have learned has been gained the hard way.

Surrendering our will to God is the only way to have a peaceful and contented life. However, the only way to lead a fulfilled life is to hold fast, with utmost determination, to the calling God has given us. It is this divine purpose that gives our lives meaning and value.

It is the struggle to know which things to surrender, and which things to hold onto, that has made my life journey so interesting--perhaps even entertaining. But in the midst of my struggling, God had a plan. With mercy and patience, He led us to Mexico to help children in need--children like Jake, whose tragic and miraculous story I have the privilege of telling in this book; children in need of a loving home and hope for the future.

We are often asked about the circumstances that caused us to leave our comfortable lives in the United States to go and serve in Mexico. People are also interested to know why we decided to adopt a Mexican teenager, and become involved in the start of a new orphanage. Even our closest friends and family don't know the whole story. So we are thankful for this opportunity to finally be able to answer all those questions.

Our "adopted son" who we call Juan in this writing has agreed to share some of his story in the hope that it will help others who are suffering as he once did. It is our hope that this will inspire you to pray for and support this ministry. All financial proceeds or donations stemming from this book will be used to help children like him-- honest children in real need here in Mexico.

While I grew up in a secure environment, Juan's childhood was the other extreme. In sharp contrast to the "American Dream" that is pretty much available in the US to anyone who studies, works hard, and plays by the rules, Mexico offers little opportunity to its people. Widespread corruption, drug-trafficking, economic instability, lack of infrastructure, and poor education standards, all contribute to making life difficult for the majority of Mexicans.

Living in the US, it is difficult to comprehend how such corruption, with the taking of bribes, can completely destroy the rule of law and order that is necessary for a healthy society. Drug trafficking lures young men to break the law because they can earn almost a year's wage in one week. Life savings are wiped out when the currency devalues and people are forced to exchange 1,000 pesos for a new currency worth only 1 peso. Schools are under-funded and unfocused. Students who do manage to get a good education, are unable to find jobs once they finish their studies. The infrastructure for industry and the economy to support good-paying jobs, are not in place.

Our neighbor to the south is a nation of approximately 100 million people of both native Indian and Spanish descent. Its culture is much older and more homogeneous than that of the US. It is also far more fatalistic. It is a country rich in natural resources, such as mineral ores and petroleum, but this wealth is concentrated in few hands.

The average family income is about 1/10th that of the average US income. Most live in poverty by US standards. Because there is no established welfare system or "safety net," some live in destitute poverty--particularly the single mothers, such as Juan's mother, and the elderly.

This is the world Juan grew up in. This is the world into which my family was moved.

We pray that you will be spiritually uplifted as you read this account--all glory be to God.

Bob Huber
February, 2006

Note: Some names have been changed.

CHAPTER ONE

* * *

Two Calls for Help

* * *

If I had my whole life to live over again,
I don't think I'd have the strength.

–Flip Wilson

I f you had told me five years ago that the plan for my life would collide with that of a needy thirteen-year-old boy in Mexico, I would have said you were crazy. Yet, in God's perfect time and wisdom, that was exactly what happened. Even during those times when I felt confused, alone, and without hope, God's eternal plans were unfolding exactly as He had determined since before the world was created....

Northwest Indiana, July 2000

The east bedroom of our large country estate was dark and quiet, but one member of the family couldn't sleep. It was 3 a.m. and I had been tossing, turning, and fully awake for five long hours. Tormented by my doubts and fears, the time had ticked slowly by--each minute feeling like an hour.

The recently built brick and limestone dream home, with its interior of custom woodwork, stainless steel, and marble, provided no comfort. Neither was the beautiful four-post cherry bed where my wife, Joy, was sleeping sweetly beside me.

My rapidly growing business held no satisfaction either. Instead, it had stolen precious time and attention away from my dear wife and two young girls.

Added to this, the sudden death of my father had robbed me of one of my closest friends and confidants.

Now all the problems and stress caused by my small business were literally giving me chest pains and anxiety attacks. I had tried to do my best, but the combination of all these trials had mounted up to an unbearable load. In the darkness of our bedroom, tears welled in my eyes as I finally prayed, "God, I just can't go on."

The admission was not easy. I was not a quitter, and had always been too proud to ever give up. But now I was desperate.

"Please help me," I begged. My heart ached and my head throbbed. I was spent, tired, broken, and ready to surrender at all costs. I had invested every ounce of myself in the business, and felt like all I had to show for it was a whole lot of pain.

"I'll go anywhere and do anything ... anything but this. Please, just get me out of this mess."

God heard my prayer, and His plan was unfolding exactly as it should. But it had taken quite a while for me to reach this point of surrender....

Mexico, December 2001

Juan had reached another low point in his turbulent young life. Slipping away from the orphanage that had become his home, he stood alone beside a mesquite tree as a wall of ominous, low, storm clouds rolled like a grey carpet across the desert sky. The brewing desert storm was a fitting backdrop for the emotions that were swirling through the boy's soul.

In the beginning, Juan had looked forward to going to the orphanage, even though it was so far away. It had been a chance for him to leave his past behind and be able to start over. It was an opportunity for him to go back to school and see a different part of the world--and when he first arrived, it had been exciting. There were the visitors from America, and all the other children to meet. There was a flush toilet, and a bed that had a mattress. While the other boys talked about running away, Juan couldn't imagine joining them. He was content to have nice clothes and shoes for the first time in his life.

In time, however, the newness wore off and Juan's heart resumed hurting once again. Thoughts of the past and all his doubts came rolling back like the dark clouds that were now brewing above him. Mysterious, troubling thoughts pushed aside the blue sky of his early excitement, as answerless questions began to plague him:

Why did my real father abandon me?
Why did my mother send me to the orphanage?
Is it true that my family does not want me?
Is there more to life than all the pain and suffering I have seen?

And then there was the greatest question of all--was there really a God in heaven who loved him?

The Christians at the orphanage had told him that this was true, but Juan wasn't sure. The boy could not understand why God would permit such pain and suffering to exist. If such a God was real, then Juan was sure that He didn't care.

It was these questions, together with all the sad memories, that tore at his young heart. "Why?" he asked, until a wave of despair finally overtook him.

In the shadow of that mesquite tree, Juan felt totally alone in the world, as if no one cared for him or wanted him. He knew that he would live out his days at the orphanage, in the same way that he had until that moment--abandoned and forgotten; little more than a punching bag for the older boys to vent their own frustrations upon.

Tiredness flooded the boy. He was tired of living with the pain and longed for it to all be over.

"Why do I have to be here?" The thought cried in his head.

Standing to his feet, Juan looked through dark, tear-blurred eyes at the astonishing sight that was building above him. Anger boiled within him like the massive clouds that were gathering overhead. It was time to confront this God who supposedly created everything, but let people suffer.

"I wanted to believe in you, and that you could help me--but you don't. So I don't believe in you!" he sobbed. "You are nothing to me, because you do nothing!"

Then, mustering all his strength, the boy let out one long, fierce scream that was filled with the pent up anguish of a life of sorrow.

Before his cry had ended, a flash of lightning filled the sky, followed immediately by a tremendous crack of thunder that completely drowned out the sound of his voice. It was so sharp that Juan instinctively ducked his head. The roar of thunder was so powerful that the sound buckled his knees, almost knocking him to the ground. It was as if God Himself was saying, "Enough is enough," as He prepared to demonstrate His power.

Staggering from the shock of the unexpected explosion, Juan was suddenly struck by a profound fear of an almighty God. The deafening thunder continued to roll on and on as it echoed off the majestic mountains that surrounded the valley. In an instant, the boy knew that there was, indeed, a God, and that he had, most likely, offended him. As this thought took hold, Juan was gripped with wide-eyed fear. Suddenly he felt like running for his life.

Trying to avoid what he believed would be the inevitable strike that would take his life, Juan crouched low and ran as fast as he could toward the dormitory. As he did, the sky lit up with fire again, and his ears rang with the sound of the thunder's awesome crack and boom.

Now running in a zigzag pattern, Juan careened even faster, his heart pounding. He arrived at the dorm, tore down the hallway and dove into his bed.

Again the thunder roared. "I am the almighty God, and I have conquered sin and death!" it seemed to say.

Juan pulled the covers over his head, curled up in a ball, and pushed himself as low as he could in his bed. "Oh, God," he panted, as large raindrops started to pelt the dormitory's metal roof and a dusty wind howled through the open window. "I'm sorry for saying that. I do believe--I mean, I want to believe in you. Please help me ... oh God, if you are there, please help me...."

God heard Juan's prayer. In fact, God already had a plan for Juan, and it had been unfolding from the day he was born. Events had been set into motion that would change his life forever.

A few days after that storm in the desert, a group of Americans arrived to work at the orphanage for a week. Among them was one extremely nervous and reluctant volunteer from 2000 miles away--me.

18

My wife and I had been called to a ministry, but we didn't know what. For two years we had been praying for direction--and now we were about to find it.

CHAPTER TWO

* * *

The Road to God's Answer

* * *

Hold fast to dreams
For if dreams die
Life is a broken-winged bird
That cannot fly.

-Langston Hughes

Growing up in the small town of Francesville, Indiana, it wasn't long before my friends and family gave me the affectionate title of "whiz kid." I earned this label because I had begun programming my own computer games at the age of eight.

Even so, "whiz-kid" or not, I never really went out of my way to extend myself. I used to think that getting "A's" and "B's" in school was good enough. After all, I could achieve those grades without having to work too hard--so why bother?

That was until one landmark day when my 5th grade teacher, Mrs. Patty, took me aside and challenged me about my attitude.

"Do you know what apathy is?" she asked, taking hold of my arm and glaring at me.

I shook my head.

"It's what you have," she stated.

"I have what?" I asked, eyes widening in horror at the prospect of having contracted some obscure disease.

"You're not doing your best," she clarified, showing me a paper I had written and pointing to the grade scribbled in red ink.

I was confused. "But I got a B+ didn't I? Isn't that good enough?" I asked.

"You can't just settle for good enough!" she shouted. "You have a great deal of potential, and with that comes a responsibility to use your talents. You are capable of doing better, and I am going to hold you accountable!"

I had a lot of respect for Mrs. Patty, and being a sensitive child who always wanted to please, I took her words to heart. From then on, I felt compelled to do my best, and started to really focus and apply myself to everything I did.

My father was also a major influence in this regard. He had always said, "It only takes a little bit longer to do the job right," and this was an attitude that I saw him put into action on a regular basis. Dad was an electrician, and I vividly remember seeing the quality work that he always did whenever he was on the job.

My experiences were forming me. An "over-achiever" was in the making.

Although I have never considered myself as being particularly intelligent, there's no question that I have been competitively determined and focused since my youth. From that day when Mrs. Patty told me that she would be holding me accountable, I have worked hard to always do every job right. In high school I didn't just shoot for an "A," I aimed for an "A+."

It was this attitude that placed me at the podium in June 1987, preparing to give the Valedictorian address at the graduation of my high school class.

Following the death of one of our classmates, Chrissy, just two days earlier in a shocking car accident, the graduation director had requested that all speeches be edited to avoid any mention of the tragedy. The hope was that by doing this we may avoid breaking down and crying in front of a thousand guests.

I still remember standing there on the platform, in front of a sea of people, with my notes full of marked-out words and handwritten changes. As I prepared to speak, the writing on the page blurred. I fought to blink back tears. A trickle of sweat ran down my back, and every beat of my heart reverberated through my body. Yet, as I stood at that podium, I felt a strange inner strength and peace.

It was a pivotal time for my classmates and me. We were about to enter the "real world;" although the "real world" had already left its mark with the cold facts of life and death. We were growing up and we needed to be strong for each other. I was determined to be the best example I could be for my friends. Although I knew I was nothing of myself, I felt a responsibility to say what I could to encourage them on their way.

I knew that I was respected by my class, and often looked to for leadership, advice or help. As well as being elected senior class president of West Central High School, I had also been voted "most-likely-to-succeed" by the 78 members of the Class of 1987. On our graduation day, I don't remember all that I said, but I know I gave a testimony of my faith in Jesus Christ, and encouraged them to never, ever, give up on their dreams.

Moving on to college, I felt the same responsibility to excel that had been with me for years. Majoring in computers and business, I graduated from Purdue University's Krannert School of Management at the top of my class, completing the two degrees in five years.

It was during my time at college that I married Joy--a beautiful, blue-eyed brunette from my hometown. Joy was also a leader amongst her peers, but her aspirations were homemaking, not business.

Finally, I graduated from Purdue University with a Master's Degree in Business Administration, after being labeled a "computer-whiz" by college faculty. Although this was an exaggeration, the lavish recommendation helped me land two prestigious summer internships--one at Discover Card in Chicago, and the other at a Big-Six technology firm in Indianapolis. Not surprisingly, I loved the challenge and threw myself into the work. By God's grace, I was able to live up to my college reputation.

After the internships, I went to work for a small manufacturing company, where I helped achieve an amazing turnaround. To some, it probably appeared as though everything I touched turned to gold. However, it had more to do with the fact that I had a one-track, problem-solving mind. I was almost always thinking about the business, to the point of even waking up at night with solutions to problems. Once a situation had been permanently solved, I would move straight onto the next.

In much the same way, I set goals in every area of my life, and regularly revisited them in order to make adjustments. Whenever I reached a goal, I would immediately reset it at a higher level. "Good enough" was never good enough for me. I was passionate about doing the very best I could, but somehow it seemed that I always reached my business-related goals more frequently than I did my personal and spiritual goals.

In 1996 I started my own high-tech business, AdaptaSoft, working from a 6 x 12 foot office in my garage in Francesville--a place that no one had ever heard of. Yet, from that small, rural town, I was selling products all around the world.

Sales and profits skyrocketed, and soon I was signing lucrative contracts with companies like Hewlett Packard, and doing business with billionaires like Michael Dupont and other industry leaders.

Before long, my small company was providing well-paying professional jobs to employees, as well as the promise of great economic benefit for my shrinking hometown.

During this time, God blessed my wife and me with two beautiful little girls, and we settled into the joys and challenges of family life. With the profits from my business, we bought 24 acres on the side of town and built a large, three-story home. Joy and I were well respected in the community and active in the church, where we served as Sunday school teachers. I was 31 years old.

We were just everyday people who came from humble families living in a small town. But, for whatever reason, we were living the American dream. Even so, some unexpected turns waited just ahead.

Anyone would think that a young couple would be extremely happy to see such success so early in life--and for a time, we were. Then things started to go wrong, as my family embarked on an exciting, but spiritually and emotionally draining, journey. Things didn't turn out as I had expected ... or as you might think.

Although 1999 ended up being the most profitable year for my company, it was also, by far, the most miserable year of my life. In that same 12 months, we would build our dream home, encounter many business problems, and worst of all, lose a dearly loved family member.

I had many lessons to learn, and it was just the beginning of a journey that would lead us from the high-tech business world in the United States, to the high-poverty world in Mexico--the last place on earth I ever thought we'd live.

This is the story of how God changed our direction and forever changed our lives.

CHAPTER THREE

* * *

The Birth of Juan

* * *

The most important thing a father can do for his children
is to love their mother.

–Reverend Theodore Hesburgh

At the age of 14, Sara was an orphan and living on her own in Navojoa. Without a mother or father to give her guidance, she had learnt life's lessons the hard way--all alone in a harsh and unforgiving world.

When Sara met strong, young Antonio, who seemed to be crazy about her, she fell immediately in love with the macho "muchacho." Within two weeks the two were living together, and Juan was conceived.

It was an exciting time for the young mother-to-be, with new experiences and sensations. But as is often the case in Mexico, the couple was unprepared for the realities of life and the responsibilities associated with raising a child.

Navojoa is an economically depressed area in Northern Mexico, about 400 miles south of the US border. Although there are more repressive areas in the world, North Americans would probably rank it in the top 10 worst places to live.

Situated in the middle of a desert, there is little rainfall and the summer temperatures regularly exceed 120 degrees. There are very few rich among the inhabitants, and many poor. Most of the streets are dirt ruts and potholes, and the air is dust and smoke.

You can bribe almost anyone for anything. Drugs can be bought on most corners and even in elementary schools. Good jobs are scarce, and most work pays the equivalent of less than one dollar an hour.

The combination of low wages and high cost of living made married life, with a newborn baby, a brutal battle for survival for the young couple.

Juan was born on November 11, 1988. Not long after that, his father, Antonio, abandoned his wife and baby.

Perhaps the young man saw no hope in his situation, or maybe he simply chose his own personal freedom over the responsibility of a wife and child. Whatever the reason, a relationship that was weak from the start--and shakier as time went by--completely fell apart with the added stress of an infant.

In an effort to justify his hasty exit, Antonio claimed that Juan was not his son. It was a lame excuse for a thoroughly selfish act, as there was no question that he was the father--the resemblance was strong.

Sara was left completely brokenhearted and destitute. At the tender age of sixteen she had the responsibility of caring for her baby alone. Without any family to fall back on, Sara knew she would have to do whatever was needed to survive.

Not long after their relationship fell apart, an argument erupted between Sara and Antonio. After that, Antonio was bent on doing whatever he could to hurt the woman he had once loved--and he knew exactly what would hurt her the most. Although Sara didn't have much in the world, she did have one very precious possession-- her son. So when she wasn't looking, Antonio stole away with Juan.

Later, Sara found her husband and demanded to know where he had taken her son. Antonio only smiled and wouldn't tell her.

Frantically she retraced his tracks. Using detective work, Sara was able to talk to several people who had seen Antonio take Juan, and they were able to tell her where he had been heading.

It was then that she heard and recognized Juan's cry. Moments later, she found her baby son thrown into a trash dumpster. Sara's heart nearly burst with the anguish of seeing her precious child lying in such squalor.

During the horrific moments after Juan disappeared, Sara had prayed like she had never prayed before. Then, once her crying child was cradled safely in her arms again, all she could do was thank God for returning Juan to her.

* * *

"With this money you can go back to school and make a life for yourself," the well-dressed man said.

"We can give him everything he will need to live a full and happy life," pleaded the woman at his side. Her manicured finger-nails gleamed in the sunlight as she wrung her hands.

Sara looked at the new car they were driving and the thick enve-lope of money they were holding out toward her.

"What do you have to offer him?" they asked.

The question made Sara think. While her friends were going to school, dressing up for parties and living carefree lives, she was working at whatever job she could find, in order to scrape together enough money to survive.

But would they survive?

Sara looked at the wealthy, childless couple from Mexico City and wondered if perhaps Juan would be better off with them. Sara was tempted, as they were offering a great deal of money, which would provide her with the opportunity to go out with boys and enjoy herself like the rest of the girls her age.

Just then Juan began to cry, as if he knew that she was thinking about selling him.

What did she have to offer him?

"My love," she said, then turned and walked away.

Juan was all she had in the world. As tempting as the offer had been, Sara knew that there wasn't any amount of money that would convince her to sell her own child.

"You're making a big mistake!" the man yelled after her.

"He is going to suffer and it will be all your fault!" The woman's accusation followed Sara down the street.

There were many times thereafter when Sara wondered if they hadn't perhaps been right. A couple of times Juan almost died of various infirmities. He would get sick, but she couldn't afford to go to a doctor. In desperation, she tried to get help from Antonio, but he demanded that she sleep with him first. Sara declined.

One time, a golf ball sized cyst grew below Juan's eye, threatening his vision. Thankfully it went away on its own. Not long after that, another cyst grew on his neck, about the size of an orange--and it continued to grow. Juan needed surgery or he would eventually suffocate and die.

Sara was desperate, and she didn't have much time.

It was during this most difficult time that Sara met Nataniel, her second husband. He was several years older, but he offered to help her and Juan. He was able to legally adopt the boy, which gave Juan medical coverage through his work.

The surgery to remove the cyst was successful and Juan showed no signs of it, other than a small scar on his neck.

Nataniel and Sara worked hard to buy a small lot on the far edge of town. There they built a one room casita out of wood timbers, scraps and cardboard. There they would have three more children.

For a time they were all happy together.

CHAPTER FOUR

* * *

The Birth of AdaptaSoft Inc.

* * *

One doesn't discover new lands without consenting
to lose sight of the shore for a very long time.

–Andre Gide

Although not as traumatic as the birth of a child, the birth of a company can be a tumultuous event. AdaptaSoft Inc. began in the summer of 1996, as an idea I presented to my first employer.

I had hesitated for a moment outside the office door of the company president, questioning whether this was really something that I was ready for. Although I had been thinking about it for a long while, I was far from certain that the time had come to pursue it. Finally, I took a deep breath, knocked on the door, and then pushed it open.

My boss, Jon, was reading at his large, cherry-wood desk, as I made my tentative entrance. Hearing my knock, he looked up and smiled.

Jon was a wonderful "people person." He was handsome, warm and sincere--the type of person you always remember meeting. He was also a Christian, and blessed with a beautiful family. Their pictures graced the walls of his newly remodeled corner office.

"Excuse me, Jon," I began. "I was wondering if I could talk to you about something."

"Sure Bob, have a seat. What's up?" My employer motioned graciously to a soft, leather chair.

Jon and I had worked together for four years, and we knew each other well. I had started working for him straight out of college. Jon had great strengths in sales and visioning. His weakness was in controlling the business and managing the details, which was why he hired me. Together, we made a great team--Jon focused on growing the business, while I focused on details and making it profitable. With God's help, we were able to turn financial strain into financial success. In four years the company had nearly tripled in size and was turning a substantial profit.

Even with that strong working relationship together, it had still been hard to say what was on my mind. In the end, I just blurted it out.

"I've been thinking about starting my own business,"

My level of discomfort increased dramatically as the smile faded from Jon's face. Without waiting for his response, I went on to explain how starting my own computer software business had been a long-time dream--one I had held since high school. Then I added, "With

34

the company doing so well now, I really think it might be a good time for me to step out."

Jon had been good to me in many ways, including my compensation. Working for him, and going through all the financially hard times, had taught me a lot about running a business. At the very least, it had removed the fear I'd always had of taking the risk of starting my own.

Originally, I had planned on staying with Jon for five years, but the differences in the way we thought had begun to wear on me. He wanted to continue to grow the company at a rapid pace, and I honestly didn't know if I could keep up--or even if I wanted to.

The thought of starting my own business was exciting, although I knew that it would be a risky move. John and I had definitely worked well together, and I was aware that by going out on my own I could very easily fail. Still, even with that risk, I was anxious to focus more time on what I saw as a great opportunity in the world of technology.

"I can honestly say that I'm not excited about thinking of you leaving," Jon finally said.

"A big part of me doesn't want to either," I admitted, thankful to know that I was appreciated.

I was proud of the success we had enjoyed together and wanted it to continue. With that in mind, I floated the idea of making a gradual move out of the company over a period of months, while stepping into my own business at the same time. It was a win-win situation.

As we talked, Jon and I worked out a plan that we hoped would be good for everyone.

Jon's willingness to help me in this way was very generous, and I will be forever indebted to him. However, I think that he was also very grateful for the help I had given him during my four years with the company. Together we had brought it back from the brink, to the point where it was turning a sizable profit.

So, with an agreement in place, I began the process of making the transition from working for a manufacturing company, to eventually forming my own software company.

* * *

By the time I made the step from employee to business owner, there had already been a steady move out of our small town by the young, the college educated, and the skilled, in search of employment.

In 1996, Francesville was home to about 800 people, and not much else in terms of good-paying jobs. The exodus was crippling both the community and our home church.

I loved our small town, and felt blessed to have grown up there. It was a quiet, peaceful, friendly place to live and raise a family. It was for this reason that I wanted to give something back in return for what I felt I had received.

From the time when, at a young age, I became a Christian, I started searching for God's purpose in my work. Because of the love I had for my hometown, I began looking for a way to reverse the trend of people leaving. The more I thought about it, the more determined I became to make a difference. Consequently one of the main goals of AdaptaSoft was to create 50 good-paying, professional-level jobs.

Even so, Francesville was not a good place to start a new business--particularly a high-tech one. It did not make good business sense to locate a software company in the middle of nowhere. But I had prayed about it, and felt that it was God's will. So, with His help, AdaptaSoft was born in Francesville, Indiana--and with what had become my characteristic discipline and determination, I threw myself into making it grow.

CHAPTER FIVE

* * *

The Complex World of Payroll

* * *

Cast thy bread upon the waters:
for thou shalt find it after many days.
In the morning sow thy seed,
and in the evening withhold not thine hand:
for thou knowest not whether shall prosper,
either this or that, or whether they both
shall be alike good.

-Ecclesiastes 11:1, 6

"Are you coming to bed soon?" Joy asked, sticking her head in the door of my garage office. Although a bit tired, she looked lovely standing there in her nightgown.

"I'm sorry sweetheart," I apologized, "but I've got this thing all torn apart and I need to get it put back together."

At that moment, I was up to my eyebrows in a complex, programming mess, which made stopping very difficult. With so many details to be juggled, the only way to handle a task of this nature was to finish it in one sitting.

"Well how long do you think it will take?"

"I don't know, probably a couple more hours."

"Honey, it's already past 11. Can't you finish it tomorrow?" The disappointment was obvious in her voice.

"No, I can't. When I'm programming like this, I'm like a submarine way underwater. I can't surface without losing my grasp on 101 details," I tried to explain. "These algorithms are so complicated that if I don't stay totally focused, I may screw them up, and not know it. Then a customer can lose a bunch of money and sue us for damages."

"I can't remember the last time we went to bed together," Joy exaggerated.

"I'm sorry," I sighed. Joy gave me a disappointed look.

"Just let me get this done, and I won't do it tomorrow," I promised.

"That's what you always say," she said in disgust, and closed the door.

Someone once said that we start our own businesses so we can work 80 hours a week for ourselves, instead of 40 hours a week for someone else. Starting AdaptaSoft meant many late nights and early mornings of intense programming. It was early in 1997--I was on my own, and working like crazy to make my business a success.

Everyone knew I had ventured out on my own, and many had said that I would never make it. "You are doing *what?!*" they would say, their mouths dropping open in astonishment.

Once again, I would try to explain our business plan--a difficult thing to do in few words--but I could see that I wasn't convincing them at all. Very quickly, I was written off as being either over-confident or just plain loony. After all, nobody started a high-tech company in Francesville--not if they hoped to succeed. Everybody seemed quite sure of that, but I felt sure that I would prove them wrong. In the process, I was determined to avoid my ultimate fear--failure.

When we went on vacation, my laptop and cell phone were always with me. I spent many hours typing and making phone calls on the hotel balcony overlooking the pool where Joy and the girls swam.

I had personally designed, developed, and programmed FlexPay, investing two arduous years of my life into its development. It was like a child, and I gave it more attention than I did to my own family.

My initial plan for starting the business was to create a complete accounting package. However, due to the complexity of the payroll aspect in any accounting program, I decided to start with that part first, because it was something that few competitors offered. My plan was to complete the payroll section and then license it to others. I would then use the profit from this portion of the program to build the rest of the accounting system. Hence, FlexPay Payroll was born.

I knew payroll was complicated, as I had done the payroll for my previous employer for years. But I hadn't realize how insanely complicated it was nationwide. I honestly had no idea just how much of a mess I was getting into.

Once I started selling my payroll product, a pattern soon developed. Customers were constantly asking for more features and functionality such as, 401k benefits, vacation day accrual, court garnishments, special overtime calculations, union payroll reports, direct deposits, special taxes, etc. It was a never ending cycle. Even though I was working very hard and programming almost constantly, I could never finish adding to the payroll program.

There were federal taxes, state and county taxes, unemployment, and social security taxes. They were all calculated differently and they all changed periodically. Consequently, as I added features, or made amendments to the taxes, all these changes had to be backward compatible, so as not to disrupt customers already using the product. To do this, I had to build a form of artificial intelligence into the software that could detect earlier versions of the program and then bring them up to the current version, without making any errors in the customer's data.

These updates had to be delivered error free, or it would lead to a nightmare of irate customers, corrupted data, and hours of technical support to correct the problems--not to mention the possibility of huge tax penalties.

All of this added up to thousands of hours of nose-to-the-computer-screen hard work--and quite honestly, it didn't seem to be paying off. The product wasn't selling all that well, and even the sales we made were for prices lower than we had hoped.

On top of the programming work, there was the issue of technical support, or helping the customer set up and use the software.

I hated technical support calls. Each time, I had to grit my teeth and try so hard not to get mad at people. They would ask, "Can you walk me through that?" which actually meant "I want you to explain, step-by-step, where to click and what to type." A whiney customer could keep me on the phone for hours, while other far more pressing, paying jobs stacked up.

Customers insisted that we provide this service free of charge, because after all, they had just purchased the software, and they wanted to get it up and running. To be fair, we could understand their side of it, because we too had purchased software from other vendors and had also expected free support. Even so, it seemed like we were spending way too much time on the phone. All too often we would find ourselves painstakingly troubleshooting their printer, or network, or something else that had nothing to do with our software, but was necessary for our program to work for them.

This was the world that I had stepped into--a world where I was working like crazy on my startup business in Francesville. In the meantime, an eight-year-old boy was working a type of business too, on the hot, dusty streets of Navojoa, Sonora

CHAPTER SIX

* * *

Growing Up in Navojoa

* * *

Tis better to suffer wrong
than do it.

-Thomas Fuller

"Fresh donuts for a peso!" the slender, eight-year-old boy called cheerfully from the dirt street, as he went door-to-door selling donuts. Juan's ragged clothes usually caused people to have compassion on him, but they hadn't helped him to sell many donuts that day.

His stepfather, with whom he was living at the time, would make the donuts in the morning, and Juan then had to sell them all before returning home. Depending on the generosity of the people on the street, he could sometimes finish early, which meant he would have time to play baseball in the afternoon. But some days, as was the case on this particular day, there would still be donuts in his basket late into the afternoon.

With what he earned, his family could buy a few eggs and tortillas, as well as the ingredients to make more donuts.

Most people ignored him, but as he persistently went door-to-door, and asked all passers-by, someone would eventually make eye contact with him. He had a broad, winsome smile, which he used to his advantage.

When Juan asked a person if they wanted a donut, they would invariably want to know who had made them. He would look the person in the eye, and say that they had been made by his grandmother. It was a lie, but the boy had learned early on that nobody bought donuts made by a stepfather.

Juan was sure that there were many times people bought his donuts, but never ate them. In fact, there were many occasions when they would just give him the peso and not take a donut at all. This brought on a bit of a dilemma because, although he appreciated the donation, the sooner he sold them, the sooner he could go home.

Of course, his stepfather was always careful to count the donuts and the money every day. If the accounting was even a peso short, Juan would receive a swift beating. With that fear in mind, he had to make sure that every donut was sold.

Even so, it didn't take Juan long to think of a solution to the problem of people paying for donuts they didn't want. He would simply eat the rejects!

On this particular day, the midday sun was very hot, and Juan's basket was still half full of donuts. Feeling discouraged by the unusually bad luck he was having, Juan's mind started to wander to thoughts of baseball.

Suddenly an angry dog jumped out at him, growling and snapping ferociously. Startled, the boy tripped and fell, sending his basket flying and donuts rolling in all directions.

For a while, Juan sat where he had fallen--dejected, discouraged, and wondering what to do next.

Finally, he picked up some rocks and threw them at the dog that was now happily eating his donuts. Then, once the dog had gone, Juan started gathering the donuts and putting them back into the basket.

The problem he had been having that morning, was now so much worse. He knew he couldn't return home without selling the whole basket, or he would get a beating--his stepfather would never believe his excuse about the dog. But who would want to buy dirt-covered donuts?

With great care, Juan began cleaning the dirt off each donut. Then, taking some of the powdered sugar he always carried, he sprinkled a little more on each donut before placing it neatly back into his basket.

Once the damaged donuts had all been repaired, Juan dusted himself off, and then went back to his job--eventually selling every one of those dirty donuts!

He finished the day without the same music in his voice, or sincerity in his smile, but he did what he knew he had to do. Like so many of the poor in Mexico, Juan was learning how to survive.

Juan was a bright, handsome boy, who was doing well in elementary school. Before long, his eye was caught by a pretty girl in one of his classes. As she lived nearby, Juan would follow her home from school. He wanted her to be his friend, but every time he tried to talk to her, she seemed to ignore him.

One day, Juan got an idea of how to win the girl over. He started saving his money to buy her a present, which took a great deal of discipline because money was always in demand. Eventually, he had saved enough to be able to buy a bag of potato chips.

That day, after school, he mustered all his willpower and went to the girl's house to deliver his gift.

Arriving on her doorstep, it was obvious to the boy that both parents had good jobs. The house was made of brick and cement; not scrap wood and tar paper like Juan's home. He looked down at his tattered, worn clothing, and thought of the nice clothes and shoes that the girl always wore. For a moment he hesitated, but then put on a friendly smile and knocked on the door.

But things did not go as Juan had hoped. To his great disappointment, the girl did not receive his gift. Her parents had told her not to associate with him because he was from a poor family.

Totally dejected and feeling very sorry for himself, Juan returned home. For a long time, the boy sat and thought about what had happened. Then he slowly opened the bag and ate the chips.

The girl was not the only person ignoring Juan. In fact, nobody paid too much attention to him. After all, he was just another skinny, dirty boy, and there were already plenty of those running around the neighborhood. Because of this, Juan looked forward each year to the one day that was just for him--his birthday. Usually, on that day, he got a little special attention or a pat on the back. Sometimes they would even sing the "mañanitas," which is the song they sing for birthdays in Mexico.

So when November 11 arrived, Juan awoke early, eager to begin making his rounds of those people who were most important in his life. But his enthusiasm and excitement soon diminished as person after person revealed that, to them, it was just another day. No one had remembered that it was his birthday.

From American Dream to God's Destiny

Finally, late in the day, he resorted to asking if anyone knew what day it was--but no one did.

When it was obvious that everyone had forgotten, he went to his grandmother, and said, "Today is my birthday."

"Oh, that's nice," she replied, before turning and walking away. It wasn't much, but that acknowledgement was all Juan received for his birthday that year.

Receiving so little attention or supervision, Juan had the freedom to go and do whatever he wanted. He had heard about the videos that were being shown secretly in a house a few blocks away. The young man who lived there alone had a TV and video player, as well as several pornographic videos. For an admission fee of 4 pesos, he would let children in to watch them. The room was usually packed.

When Juan's friends told him about all the incredible things they had seen there, he wanted to see them for himself. He didn't understand it all, but his friends' fascination made him curious. Four pesos was a fortune for Juan, but by doing odd jobs and trading various toys, he managed to get the money together.

A dozen young boys packed into the dark room. All were excited, eyes fixed to the TV screen as the scenes unfolded.

Juan was shocked by what he saw. The film went on and on--the images burned forever into his young mind. In that one moment, his innocence was shattered.

46

CHAPTER SEVEN

* * *

Payroll Bob

* * *

The trouble with life in the fast lane is that
you get to the other end in an awful hurry.

–John Jenson

"Hi, I'm Bob ... or 'Payroll Bob' as they call me," I chuckled as I offered my hand. I had never met a billionaire before, and was feeling a little nervous.

"Oh, Bob, yes I've heard about you. Nice to meet you," he said with a smile.

There was something very unassuming about the man. Dressed as he was in casual clothes, he appeared just like any other person. In fact, to look at Michael Dupont, you would never know that he was the son of the chairman of the global Dupont Company.

It was 1998 and I was working in Oceanside California as a consultant for CyberOffice, a new company that Michael had formed to develop and market a new accounting software. I made several trips there to help with the payroll part of the project, and it was an interesting and exciting experience--not to mention, they paid me extremely well. One time I flew the whole family out with me, and they put us up in a beachfront apartment for two weeks.

Because FlexPay was still not paying the bills, I needed to find a way to make the business cash flow. One area I found was in providing custom consulting, or custom programming. Companies, like CyberOffice, would call with problems and ask me to help them find a solution. Although some companies found the cost of my service too high, many more were willing to pay $100 per hour, or more, for my time--and considered it good value. Some of the jobs were relatively small programs, that only took a few minutes for me to do, but ultimately saved the customers much time and money.

I soon found that doing this type of consulting, on top of my other programming, made us more money than the sales of FlexPay and everything else combined. For example, CyberOffice alone paid me as much as $7500 per week.

Incidentally, Michael Dupont's startup never made it off the ground. Eventually, our business relationship expired, along with his accounting software dream and over 12 million dollars he had invested.

It was around this time that one of my customers, Sam, made a suggestion.

"Bob, have you ever thought about selling your product to payroll service bureaus?" he asked one evening, as we talked over the phone.

The clock on the office wall showed that it was 11:05 pm, and as usual, I was still hard at work on both FlexPay and a consulting project.

"No ... not really," I replied. "What do you mean?"

To be honest, I didn't even know what a payroll service bureau was, but was too embarrassed to admit it.

"I think your product would be a good fit," Sam explained. "There aren't any good products out there in Windows. And with Y2K coming up, there are sure to be many bureaus changing from DOS to Windows' products. Seems like a great opportunity for you."

"Well, what would you suggest we do?" I was looking for opportunities, because at that point, FlexPay seemed to be going nowhere fast.

"You'd need to add more features for the service bureau--you know, ways for them to automate processing, handle trust funds, tax forms, and so forth."

It sounded interesting, so I finally leveled with him. "Forgive me, Sam, but can you explain what you mean by a service bureau?"

"Well sure. A payroll service bureau is simply a company that does payroll for other companies."

Sam went on to explain that these bureaus created payroll checks for the employees of other companies. They did all the paperwork, paid the taxes, filed the forms, and delivered a package containing the actual payroll checks to the customer.

This service allowed small and midsized businesses a way to avoid the complexities of payroll, as well as the very real possibility of tax penalties for errors. It struck me as a fantastic idea!

Studies showed that, over time, the average company would pay more in tax penalties than they would have paid in fees to have a payroll service provided. So, ultimately, this type of service saved the customer time and money. It was no wonder that people weren't exactly snatching up our FlexPay payroll program!

By the time I hung up the phone, I was already thinking about the possibilities. With Y2K approaching, and the fact that there was not a lot of competition, it looked like an opportunity we couldn't pass up.

Within days I had decided to create a new version of FlexPay, specifically for payroll service bureaus--but I needed help. I was already too busy with programming and consulting work to take on anything else by myself. So I hired my first employee.

Tim was a bright, hard working, 18-year-old--completely inexperienced, but a fast learner, as well as totally dedicated and honest. Together we dove into this huge, new project.

We named the new version, CyberPay, and there were many features we needed to add. So we started programming, and created two new products--one a remote product, and the other a tax reporting module, called CyberTax.

It was another great undertaking, but we were excited about the potential of this new market for our product. Up until this time, we hadn't made any significant money from our original program, FlexPay, which was selling at a sales price in the hundreds. The hope was that CyberPay, with a sales price in the thousands, would prove to be far more profitable.

At last it looked as though things were coming together in my world ... just as the world of 10-year-old Juan was falling apart.

CHAPTER EIGHT

* * *

A World Collapses

* * *

Loneliness and the feeling of being unwanted
is the most terrible poverty.

–Mother Teresa

The two sat alone, in silence, on the side of the small, wooden bed. Sara ran her fingers through Juan's short-cropped hair. He sat hunched over; his ribs showing through a too small T-shirt.

"I know it might be difficult for you to understand, but I thought it was time that you knew," she said.

Juan sat, stoop-shouldered, trying to comprehend what his mother had just told him--Nataniel was not his real father. So many questions raced through his mind. Was this some kind of joke? What did it mean? Who was his real father? Where was he?

Juan was quick on his feet and had a sharp mind. No one had ever come right out and told him about sex, but based on what he had seen in the movies, together with the things his friends had told him, he had been able to put it all together. For the first time, he understood that his mother had been with a different man.

"Who is my real father?" Juan whispered so quietly that Sara hardly heard him.

"His name is Antonio," she said, and then went on to explain how she had been very young when she had met his father. Then she told Juan how Antonio had left them.

"Nataniel is the real father of my sisters?" the boy asked.

Sara nodded and answered, "Yes."

With each answer, Juan seemed to sink even lower, and his shoulders began to shake.

"You mean that my father is not my real father," he sobbed, "and my sisters are not my real sisters!"

Juan's mind was swimming. Sara tried to comfort him, but he heard nothing more. His whole world had just fallen apart. He pulled himself away from his mother, and then just ran, and ran, and ran.

After that day, Juan's life was never to be the same. Nataniel was not his real father, and Juan knew all too well what that meant. He finally understood why there had been so many arguments in the past. Now he knew what those arguments were about. The yelling and angry words continued--there were no secrets in their one room shack.

Every time there was a fight, Juan became more depressed and angry. He felt as though he was the cause, and started to believe that if it weren't for him, everyone would get along.

Although Juan's world had changed forever, life continued on. As gas was expensive, most families cooked over a wood fire--and Juan's family was no exception. With such a high demand for fuel by so many people, wood was very scarce--and finding that wood was a major task. It involved long trips into the desert, surrounding mountains, and river valleys, where burnable wood could still be found.

Juan would go with Nataniel on these wood gathering trips. Returning home from one such trip, Juan was transporting a large bundle of sticks on the back of a bicycle. The wood was heavy and the bicycle a little big for him. He lost his balance and fell, sending the wood scattering. A tired and frustrated Nataniel exploded in anger, telling Juan that he was useless and good for nothing--words that the boy would never forget.

Arriving back at the house, Nataniel started to beat his stepson, but this time Juan tried to fight back. His featherweight frame was powerless against Nataniel's overwhelming size. Juan landed blows, but they had no affect.

Some time later, Juan sat alone, turning a knife over and over, in his hands. All he could think about was how sweet it would be to stick it deeply into the chest of his stepfather. Then he'd stick it in again, and again, while Nataniel screamed in pain. He was going to do it too, the first chance he got.

Such was the hatred that Juan had for his stepfather. He hated the unfair way that Nataniel favored his daughters, but was so strict and unmerciful with him. Yet, it was the yelling and beatings that really incensed him. Whenever Juan returned home late at night after playing video games, Nataniel would use an old fan-belt from the car to whip the boy as hard as he could.

It was during this time that Juan promised himself that he would never let another person lord over him. He vowed that he would not submit to the authority of another man. He would fight first and win ... or die trying.

For Sara and Nataniel, it was a constant struggle to provide enough for the family to eat, let alone send four children to school. To make matters worse, Nataniel refused to pay for any of Juan's expenses, because he wasn't his son. This caused even more conflict in the home.

Eventually, discouraged by the difficulty of finding work, and the pitifully low pay when he did, Nataniel stopped working altogether.

Sara suddenly had to take on the sole responsibility of raising the family and providing for their needs--but her efforts were futile. Before long, in desperation, she felt she had no choice but to start looking for another man. In the meantime, the angry arguments at home escalated. The family was being torn apart, and Juan felt responsible.

The boy was overwhelmed with feelings of helplessness and rejection, and with every passing day he became more and more rebellious. As the beatings intensified, so too did Juan's anger, guilt and depression.

Then came the day when Sara returned home to find her son lying in a puddle of his own blood.

CHAPTER NINE

* * *

Extreme Competition

* * *

I don't know the key to success,
but the key to failure is to try to please everyone.

–Bill Cosby

A year had passed since the 1998 launch of our first version of CyberPay, and although we only had about ten customers, the program was successfully calculating hundreds of payrolls all across the United States-- handling millions of dollars of federal, state and local tax dollars. CyberPay was making payments via direct deposit and electronic funds transfer, automatically filing tax forms, and printing benefit and garnishment checks.

The process of handling as many as 100 payrolls in a single office, involved a mind-boggling level of complexity--and we had built a software program to help manage it all. Every aspect of payroll, including tax payments and reporting, is time sensitive and requires perfect accuracy. We very quickly found ourselves in a highly competitive and demanding business, and there were often days when I found myself asking, "What have we gotten ourselves into!"

By the spring of 1999, we were in a race to improve CyberPay. The customers were out there, but our product was never quite complete enough to attract them--and we weren't the only payroll software company to see the Service Bureau opportunity. As it turned out, the competition was far greater, and more intense, than we had ever anticipated.

AdaptaSoft had grown to the point of having six fulltime employees. As a result, our small office in downtown Francesville was very cramped and constantly abuzz with activity. Three of us were almost completely dedicated to programming CyberPay, and we released version after version of the software. Each new version contained hundreds of changes and new features, and every change required updating the user manual and retraining of existing users. Still, our customers kept asking for more improvements and extra features to meet their needs.

The monthly cost of paying my employees was $25,000. Some months we did not sell anything, which would leave our books showing a $25,000 loss. Other months we would sell several copies of CyberPay, and make $50,000. Living with the constant extremes of feast or famine was wearing on my emotions.

As if that situation wasn't scary enough, I could see an even bigger challenge waiting for us just down the road.

The company was in a "catch-22" situation. We needed more money to create a new Internet-based version of CyberPay. Our competition was fierce, and rival companies were already working on, or coming out with, the next generation products. To remain competitive, AdaptaSoft needed to grow. To grow, we needed to make more sales. To make more sales, we had to improve our product. Catch-22.

We didn't know what we were going to do.

Then one day, a good friend of my dad came to visit. We sat outside my office, in his pickup truck, and talked.

"Bob, I believe in what you're doing here," he began. "I don't understand your business, but I know your father. I know the way he worked and the type of person he is, and I see the same qualities in you." He paused for a moment, then continued. "If your business is like most new businesses, you could use some money to help make it grow."

"It's interesting that you say that, because we do find ourselves at somewhat of a crossroad," I admitted. "We face strong competition in our market, and the other companies are much larger, and have far greater resources to draw on to develop products faster. Unless we get bigger, we may not be able to compete long term."

"Well I'm here to tell you that I trust your dad. He believed in me and my business, and he stuck with me when others didn't. In the end we were successful, and I have your dad partly to thank for it."

"I know Dad thinks a lot of you too," I said.

"To make a long story short, Bob, I'm prepared to loan you up to two million dollars to use in your business however you like. I have no doubt that you will be successful," he said with a big smile.

I was overwhelmed by the offer, but finally managed to respond, "I don't know what to say. I am deeply humbled by your confidence in me. This is something that we will need to think through."

"Well, take your time and let me know."

I wish I could say that I had as much confidence in myself as this generous man did. As I thought about using someone else's money, I just didn't feel comfortable. I was already too busy and feeling like I was in over my head. Regardless of the pros and cons of taking this investment capital, I never did seriously consider it. Then Y2K came along and it looked like the break we had been looking for.

It was no secret that the year 2000 was presenting our industry with a huge opportunity. There were several DOS based systems out there that were becoming obsolete. For example, one very popular system, RapidPay, was not year 2000 compliant, and the owner had made it known that they were not going to fix the problem. Therefore, all the RapidPay customers needed to change software before the end of the year.

We would have been an obvious choice--except that our software was new, it didn't have a proven track record, and still lacked the proven functionality of the older DOS products. RapidPay had been developed and perfected over 20 years. It had benefited from a large customer base, and was full of hidden and specialized features that its users depended on.

CyberPay was Windows based and Y2K compliant. It represented a huge development effort and had incredible functionality, but the simple fact was that there was no way we could duplicate two decades of refinement in the short time we had available. We couldn't magically recreate features that we didn't even know existed.

There were over a hundred RapidPay customers who would need to change their software before the turn of the century. With that in mind, we made it our priority to market our product to this tight-knit group. To do that, we needed to find a RapidPay user who would be able to help us make CyberPay a good fit for RapidPay customers.

Then, along came Dakota.

This company needed to convert from RapidPay, and was willing to work with us so that we could incorporate the features they needed from the current RapidPay program. Dakota also promised to recommend us to the other users in their group, dependent on such things as a smooth conversion process. They were eager to get started, and so were we. We knew that if we could satisfy Dakota, we would be able to do the same for a good number of RapidPay's other customers. The potential in sales for us was huge.

Dakota purchased CyberPay quickly--almost too quickly.

Unbeknown to us, Dakota had ulterior motives in purchasing CyberPay, and we were about to fall into a trap. Their eagerness was nothing more than a last ditch effort to try and save their largest customer. We didn't realize that Dakota was not acting in good faith.

The reality was that they had bought CyberPay quickly because they did not have any other options. Dakota's competitor had apparently purchased our competitor's software, Millennium Payroll, which was a Windows version that was, at that time, better than our own software. Dakota's main customer was planning to switch to their competitor because they wanted to use the new Millennium Payroll software--something that Dakota could not provide. Dakota had been prevented from purchasing the Millennium software because it was being sold via exclusive territories.

As to all this, we were completely in the dark, and set about working to make the improvements to CyberPay, in order to meet Dakota's needs.

The agreed plan was that we would start converting Dakota's easiest payroll customers first; in other words, those with few employees and very simple payrolls. CyberPay was quite capable of handling these simple payrolls without any modifications. However, instead of working with this plan, Dakota attempted to convert their largest customer first, which had an extremely complicated payroll.

As soon as we finalized the contract, Dakota immediately began demanding that we include tons of new features, as soon as possible. Of course, by then, we were quite used to adding new features to the program. However, the demands being made by Dakota were impossible to meet.

We did everything we could to add these features as quickly as possible. Within a few short months, incredible improvements were made to the CyberPay program, in our genuine effort to satisfy our customer's requirements. We were completely committed to making the software work for them because our own future depended on it.

We were so busy working that we didn't stop to think about what was really going on.

CHAPTER TEN

* * *

A Tragic Turn

* * *

The lowest ebb is the turn of the tide.

-Henry Wadsworth Longfellow

It was right in the middle of this time when we were struggling to satisfy Dakota, that disaster struck. It was April 1999, and I was extremely busy. Not only was I working long hours at AdaptaSoft, but we were also in the process of building our new home. Anyone who has ever built a custom home knows how consuming that process can be. There were 101 decisions to make, and we were staining trim, doors and windows late into the night.

During the height of this activity, I happened to be driving by my parent's house, one sunny day, and noticed that my dad's truck was there. I felt an urge to stop, and attributed this to the fact that I really needed some time to unwind with the two people who had always been an oasis of comfort and strength in my life. But I was running an errand and didn't think I had the time to visit--so drove on.

Even so, something kept bugging me and making me wish that I had stopped. Eventually, I promised myself that I would drop in on the way back to the office.

Pulling into the driveway, later that day, I was pleased to see that Dad's truck was still there. But a minute later, that pleasure turned into a strange sense of foreboding--their car was gone and no one was home. I knew that something was wrong.

The lunch dishes were still on the table, and it looked as if Mom and Dad had just left everything and walked out the door. Then I noticed the phone book on the table, with the page open at the number for the doctor's office. A sense of fear gripped my stomach as I grabbed the telephone and dialed the number.

As soon as I told the receptionist who I was, she put me straight through to the doctor's room. Before I had time to process what was happening, Dr. Halenburg came on the line.

"Bob ... I'm so sorry. I don't quite know how to tell you this," he began, the emotion obvious in his voice. "Your father has just passed away."

The words continued, sympathetic and caring, but I could hardly comprehend what was being said.

"Your mother is here with us, and I think it would be good if you were able to come and be with her."

"Of course ... I'll come straight away. Let her know I'll be there soon." I could hear the words, but they seemed to be coming from somewhere outside of myself. It was impossible to believe that this was happening. Dad hadn't been sick. He was still active and full of life. How could he possibly be dead?

Then I realized that I could hear my mom weeping in the background. I could picture her there in the arms of the nurses as they tried to comfort her. Suddenly my legs went weak.

It was surreal. Just like that, Dad was gone.

Dr. Halenburg told me to call the undertaker, and then to come over with him. So, in a cloud of disbelief, I looked up the number for the undertaker, and then I went riding in a hearse.

On the way, we passed by our home building site. I could see the cement trucks there pouring the foundation. I couldn't imagine ever enjoying that house without my dad. In an instant, it had lost all its appeal.

Arriving at the doctor's office, I saw that Mom's car was parked in front, with Dad slumped in the passenger seat. I opened the door, touched his cold hand, and told him one more time how much I loved him. I remembered, and was thankful, that the last time I had seen him alive I had told him the same thing, and had given him a bear hug, as was my custom.

Mom was still crying in the arms of two nurses and our family doctor. At that instant, I decided I would not think of myself, but would focus on helping my mother through this difficult time.

She was so strong, and said that she was thankful to have been with him when he died in the car. Later she told me that she had just kept saying, "I love you," over and over again.

The funeral was a blessing because hundreds of people said what a wonderful public servant my father had been. I was just beginning to understand what it meant to be a servant.

My dad had been a fortress for me--a rock that I could count on. I had always trusted his advice, and had never doubted his love. After he died, I could clearly remember my last conversations with him, our last walk, our last hug. I couldn't feel sorry for myself. In fact, I wouldn't, because I knew that I had been blessed with the most wonderful father in the world.

Even so, it was a very emotional time, with trying to be strong for Mom and the family, while dealing with such urgent problems at work. We were in the process of pouring the foundation for our new home, and at the same time, fighting to save Dakota--our all-important customer.

How I missed Dad. I needed that solid rock in my life more than ever. Without him during this difficult time, I felt more insecure. A dark cloud of fear and foreboding settled over me, dimming my outlook on everything. I started to dread going to work. The stress and pressure were building, and I even started to withdraw from Joy and the girls.

CHAPTER ELEVEN

* * *

The Trap

* * *

When the mouse laughs at the cat,
there is a hole nearby.

–Nigerian proverb

"Are you Robert Huber?" the county sheriff asked after walking into my office.

"Yes," I responded hesitantly, taking in the uniform, badge and gun belt, and wondering why he wanted me.

"This is for you," he said, handing me a thick envelope. Then he turned around and left.

The contents of that envelope sent me reeling into a world of anger and hatred that I never knew existed until that point in my life.

I had just been served court papers informing me that Dakota was suing us to reclaim all the money they had paid for our software. They were also demanding damages and lost revenues, which they claimed were a result of losing their main customer. Their argument was that the features we had freely added on to CyberPay, for their benefit, were really flaws in the program, and that these faults had caused them to lose their most valuable customer.

I was shocked and deeply hurt by the accusation. Coming, as it did, on top of my father's death, and all the pressures at work, it was more than I could take.

A few days before my father died, he had encouraged me to always take care of my most important customers--and I had taken that advice to heart. Even though Dakota's demands had continued to increase unreasonably, I was still prepared to commit every spare hour to meeting their requirements, in an attempt to keep them satisfied. Every Sunday afternoon I could be found alone in the office, programming feverishly, and I had even continued to work non-stop during the time around Dad's funeral. I had made a personal commitment to do whatever was necessary to please Dakota, seeing it as a "do or die" situation for AdaptaSoft.

My focus was so intense that one day I left work for lunch, only to discover that my car had been running in the parking lot all that morning.

Finally it reached the point where I was trying to do way too much and could not deliver totally bug-free versions of our improved software. Despite our best efforts, a few bugs escaped and caused a great deal of problems for all of our existing customers. This made a bad situation almost unbearable.

Up until this time, we had been working with Dakota on a day-by-day basis. Then one day they stopped calling--and we didn't know why. It was an eerie silence. At that point we didn't know anything about the main customer they were trying to save, or why they were so desperate to add features so quickly. We were just completely focused on trying to meet their needs. Then they sprang the law suit.

I wrote a letter to Dakota, pleading with them to reconsider. We needed to make the software work for them, and we still believed we could. But before we had a chance to do that, Dakota broke our contract and was adamant that we were at fault.

In the end, our involvement with Dakota was far from the positive reference within the RapidPay group that we had hoped it would be. In fact, it became a huge negative, and actually prevented us from reaching 100 potential customers. Being able to sell CyberPay to this specific group had been the boost that we were counting on to get us over the hump.

It was September 1999, and time was running out. Without the RapidPay customers, it was starting to look as though AdaptaSoft was finished as a company.

CHAPTER TWELVE

* * *

Uncharted Emotional Territory

* * *

No man can think clearly when his fists are clenched.

–George Jean Nathan

"**B**ob, I have good news. We have decided to go with you for the international payroll conversion," Rachel, the HP business unit manager, informed me over the phone.

"Rachel, that *is* good news!" I exclaimed--and it was. The HP contract was worth hundreds of thousands of dollars. "We will look forward to working with you."

"I will be signing the contract and mailing it back to you, but I just wanted to call and let you know."

"Thank you very much! I really appreciate your call."

"We want you to know that we are putting a great deal of trust in you and your team," Rachel admitted, before explaining further. "We chose AdaptaSoft because you demonstrated the best understanding of our problem and made the best recommendation. The price quote you gave was about the same as the rest, but none of the others could give us concise and accurate answers to our questions like you did."

"Well we are going to work very hard to prove that you have made the right choice," I assured.

During our time of crisis, this lucrative consulting relationship with HP was a blessing that literally saved us. Even so, when our sales representative first came to me and asked if I wanted to talk to HP about writing a payroll program for them, I almost said no-- after all, we were so busy working on CyberPay, there wasn't really time for anything else. However, we had reached the point where we didn't have the luxury of pouring more dollars into CyberPay, without making money on consulting as well.

I took HP's call that day, and it turned into our biggest, most profitable relationship ever. It is ironic that the things we planned for AdaptaSoft actually made us very little money, and those things we didn't plan, turned out to be more profitable.

At that time, we were not receiving enough revenue from FlexPay or CyberPay to be self supporting. Without the extra income from consulting, we would have been out of business. There is no question that God was looking out for us.

As it turned out, we were able to do a really good job for HP's Year 2000 project--even though we didn't have much time to complete it. The job was quite complicated and, obviously, it was very important that it be done right. HP had confidence in us because, by that time, I had learned quite a bit about payroll. I had quoted the project high, but they still gave us the business.

We completed the project on time, and the customer was satisfied. The revenue from this one customer represented almost all of our profits for that year. Instead of going out of business, we had our most profitable year by far.

It was a huge positive in a year of negatives, and we sure needed it. With the Dakota disaster, I have to admit that I had reached my lowest point.

For the time being, in spite of the RapidPay PR disaster, AdaptaSoft was doing well. Even so, the Dakota dispute was still eating at me. I was worried about the company's survival once the HP contract expired, and wasn't sure that we had any future outside of my consulting work.

Although AdaptaSoft had six employees, I was still responsible for all the accounting, payroll, and general management, as well as programming full time. We were growing so fast in our efforts to keep up with the competition, that there was not enough time to take a breath and refine the operation--and I was getting tired of carrying too much of the load.

As we learned more about Dakota's deliberate misleading and manipulation, I was shocked and incensed. In reality, they had been going to lose their main customer all along, regardless of what software they were using. We had worked ourselves sick trying to help them, and been duped into joining them in what was a failed attempt from the outset.

I felt foolish for not having seen it, but had been too eager to make the sale and grow the business. Then, in the end, they blamed us for their problem and wanted us to pay for their damages. The thought infuriated me--what about our damages? I felt that Dakota had gotten us into this problem, and the bad PR was costing us dearly. My anger with them was palpable.

I knew that I had entered uncharted emotional territory. Never in my life had I felt such hatred before. In the past, whenever a minister had preached that we should "love everyone," I always felt like I came pretty close. Although there were people that I disliked, I found that I could even love them, in a way. But this situation, with a customer that had been deceptive and then sued us for damages, was different. I hated these people for what they had done; not only to my company, but even more for the hurt and embarrassment they were causing me personally.

In my youth, I had gotten into a few fights with other kids at school, and had felt a lot of anger against those opponents. Like most kids, I had also fought with my siblings and even said, in childhood disgust, "I hate you." But I had never *really* hated anyone. The new feeling I was experiencing was deep, burning, and captivating.

I had taken the accusations of dishonesty personally, and even though I knew it was wrong, I couldn't escape it. I knew that the Bible said that we should forgive and turn the other cheek, but I just couldn't come to terms with this truth, or bring myself to accept it. I wanted to prove the other side wrong, and myself right. I was obsessed with setting the record straight; with not losing ... with not giving up.

We had acted in good faith, and I was determined to prove it. Unfortunately, these things are extremely difficult to prove in court, especially if your opponent has deep pockets and is not afraid to lie and obstruct. Even so, I decided to fight the accusation in court, instead of settling out of court. It was a decision that went against the advice of both my attorney and employees.

In retrospect, it was a bad decision. But at the time I felt that giving in would be the same as admitting that we had done something wrong--and I wasn't about to do that.

So we celebrated the new millennium with the successful completion of the HP contract, but still under the cloud of the Dakota dispute.

CHAPTER THIRTEEN

* * *

The Point of Surrender

* * *

I have been driven to my knees many times
because there was no place else to go.

-Abraham Lincoln

1 a.m., 2 a.m., 3 a.m. I lay awake, unable to sleep, as the hours passed slowly by.

1999 had been AdaptaSoft's best year, with the highest sales and profits of our four years in business. But now as we entered the new millennium, we were faced with circumstances and realities that would either make or break us.

The lawsuit, along with the strain of a growing business, the death of my father, and the building of our dream home, had made 1999 the most miserable year of my life. Although there were many positive things that happened during that year, the negatives far outweighed them, leaving me feeling as though the world was crashing down around me.

I was overwhelmed by the pressure, and terrified of what would happen if we failed. The question of how we would continue to serve our customers plagued my thoughts. They did the payroll for hundreds of companies, and depended on us for their critical payroll functions. Any interruption to their payroll service would result in huge financial liabilities.

As well as concern for our customers, I was also worried about the welfare of our employees, who depended on us for their livelihood. They needed their weekly paychecks, whether we made money or not. Some months we made good money, while others we lost a great deal. It was an emotional roller coaster.

Being a valedictorian in high school and at the top of my class in college, I always thought that people had high expectations for me. Even more so, I had high expectations for myself. I had been pushing myself for so long, with such an incredible fear of failure, that it's little wonder I felt as though my whole world was at stake and that everyone was watching. We were living the American dream; we had it all ... but it seemed like it could implode at any moment.

I wasn't sleeping well at night, and I couldn't concentrate during the day. I was working long hours, six days a week, and some-times Sunday afternoons. I had done my very best to satisfy all our customers, but it never seemed like it was enough. I was trying to satisfy our employees, but they never seemed happy. I was trying to make our town proud of us and of what we were doing, but instead some seemed jealous of our success and delighted by our setbacks.

It came to a head on that sleepless night, when I finally realized that I just couldn't take it any more. At last, I broke down and cried. Then, through my tears, I prayed. Over the course of that longest night, I surrendered the company and my future to the Lord. I said, "Whatever you want me to do, I'll do it. Just get me out of this painful life."

I felt trapped and wanted to dedicate my life to something that had lasting value. I was ready to surrender--or at least beginning to surrender my work to the Lord....

* * *

"I don't know how to say this other than to just say it," Tim said, as we flew home from a payroll show in Las Vegas.

"The other employees and I have been talking," he continued. "We can see that you aren't happy running the company. We would like to talk to you about a plan to buy it from you."

Many thoughts went through my head at that moment. At first I was surprised, then elated at the thought of being free from the company, but this was followed by doubt as to whether it was the right thing to do. Only a few days had passed since I surrendered AdaptaSoft to God, and now it appeared that He was giving me a way to show that I was really ready to let go. Although it seemed to be the opportunity I was looking for, something held me back.

With a forced smile, I finally responded, "I'll think about it ... we'll pray about it."

I had a weekend to ponder the pros and cons of turning the company over to my employees. I really, really wanted to, and everything within me said to get out at all cost. I wanted to do something different with my life--something with eternal benefits; something that would help someone else. There was so much competition in the payroll business that I had started to believe that the last thing the world needed was another payroll program.

But there were a few problems. For one thing, I didn't have much confidence in my employees' ability to run the company. After all, surely no one would be able to manage AdaptaSoft as well as I did--right? Then there was the hurdle of being seen as running from a problem. I was not a quitter, and did not want to be perceived in that way. However, the biggest problem of all was that I couldn't surrender the hatred I had for Dakota, nor the desire to prove myself right and them wrong.

To say that I was a little preoccupied that weekend, would be an understatement. Even at the dinner table, my thoughts were almost completely consumed with my employees' proposal.

"Did you even taste it?" Joy's words seemed to come drifting to me from a faraway place, but she was really sitting right next to me at the table.

"What did you say?" I asked, still looking out the large picture window at our backyard and trees in the distance.

"Did you even taste the food?" she repeated. "You gobbled it down so fast."

"I'm sorry. It's just that my mind is on work."

"What else is new?" Joy responded, matter-of-factly. Then, returning to her original topic, she asked, "So, was it good?"

"Delicious!" I said, forcing a weary smile.

"I can't go on like this," Joy admitted.

"I can't either," I whispered.

"You don't talk to me," she continued. "You're always in your own little world."

I cringed, knowing that she was right.

"I'd like to help you, but I don't know what's going on," Joy said. "How can I pray for you if I don't know what's happening?"

"You're right. It's just that I want so bad to sell AdaptaSoft, but...."

"Then sell it!" Joy interrupted. "Nothing is worth what you are going through. We don't need the money, and I never wanted this big house!" She gestured to the custom woodwork, brass chandelier, and two-story fireplace. It was beautiful, but it meant nothing if it was to cost us our peace and happiness.

"It's not about money," I said, shaking my head. "I just don't trust them to be able to run the company. If I thought they could pull it off, I'd turn it over to them in a heartbeat."

"Well I still say you have to do something different," Joy advised, as she stood to clear the table. "We're here ... but you aren't."

"I will try," I said. "I'm not a quitter, and I know that it will get better soon." Then, having said that, I grabbed Joy's arm, looked her in the eye, and added, "I promise."

Unfortunately, because of my pride, I couldn't bring myself to do what I really wanted to do. Even though I had no peace about it, I forced myself to make the decision to see the company and CyberPay through until everything was stable and safe enough to turn over.

After a weekend spent considering all my options, I met with my employees on the Monday, and very firmly told them "NO." I also said that they were not to waste any more time thinking about it. They were noticeably discouraged ... and I was still miserable.

Over the next few weeks, I realized that I had made a mistake. After telling my employees that I wouldn't sell the company, our relationship took a big turn for the worse, and the tension between us was growing. Some were threatening to leave, and if one or more of them did, AdaptaSoft would be sunk. Because we were such a small company, we depended on every person for so much. The loss of any of our employees would have made an already difficult situation an impossible one.

It was then that God brought back to mind the original plan I had when I first started AdaptaSoft, which was to sell the company to my employees after five years in business. At this point, we had been in operation for over four years. I then realized that there would never be a perfect time to sell, but at this point the company still had the HP support contract, and the cash flow was good.

I also remembered my commitment to surrender, and had to question whether I really meant what I had said on that sleepless night. More importantly, I had to decide whether I was ready to let go.

By this time I had started to feel that I was not cut out for running a big business. It required so much effort, and no one really seemed to appreciate that.

At last I started to understand that it might be better to swallow my pride and surrender AdaptaSoft. The development phase of CyberPay was almost over and all our customers were saying that it was getting close to being a competitive product. We were reaching the time for documentation, training, service and support--all the things I didn't enjoy as much as creating and programming.

As I thought of all these things, I started to realize that my employees probably could handle this next phase of the company just as well, if not better, than me.

CHAPTER FOURTEEN

* * *

Life on the Streets

* * *

He who has health has hope,
and he who has hope has everything.

–Arab proverb

Following Juan's attempt to end his life, his family realized how much the conflict in the home was affecting him. They searched for a solution, looking for another option for the boy, and found one. Juan went to live with the grandparents who had agreed to take him in--his biological father's parents.

He stayed with his grandparents for a while, then later lived with his uncle who was single. There are things about this time in Juan's life that are too personal to share. Even now, he finds it difficult to talk about some events during this period--and understandably so. However, it appears that he moved from place to place, never really having anywhere to call home. From time to time he would return to be with his mother, only to leave home again when the same conflicts returned.

By the time Juan reached the fifth grade, he decided that he didn't want to go to school anymore. So he dropped out and started to work at various odd jobs in order to buy food. He worked as a helper for a plumber, and also in an auto-body shop, sanding cars.

Money was always short, and Juan was almost always hungry. Sometimes, in the middle of the night, his uncle and he would steal chickens from their neighbor's yard. Then they would prepare them and cook them over an open fire. Chicken never tasted so good.

When Juan was hungry, he would also steal food from stores. If he had a few pesos to buy something, he would stuff several items into his pants, and then just pay for one of them at the checkout.

One day, Juan was caught stealing, and he was sure that he would be sent to jail. But when the staff took him to the back room, they asked if there was anything else he needed--and then, moved with compassion, they gave it to him. After that, they told him not to steal anymore, and sent him on his way.

At times, Juan also resorted to eating lizards, frogs, and rabbits, cooking them over an open flame. Life for him, as a child often living alone on the street, was a matter of survival.

Juan had a lot of time on his hands--time to think about why neither his real father nor stepfather had wanted him, and time to think about all the problems with his mother and home. He also had a lot of time to wander the streets and make friends with other men--both young and old. Juan liked to sing, and was good at it. The men enjoyed sitting around smoking, drinking beer, and listening to him sing. One man shoved a beer in his hand and said, "Here, drink this so that you smell like a man."

Listening to the radio, Juan soon memorized more than a hundred songs. Then, in his clear, boyish voice, he would sing a song with gusto, and receive the adoration of his audience. Sometimes they would toss him a coin, or a beer, or a cigarette, but what Juan really loved was the attention and praise.

He began to spend a lot of time singing for the men, and soon started to join in the smoking and drinking. He even began to experiment by drinking beer and smoking marijuana at the same time. Not surprisingly, there were times when he became intoxicated.

By the time Juan was 11, he was spending even more time on the street, where he was learning all kinds of things. Drugs were everywhere, and the boys his age, older boys and even grown men he knew--were using them. Soon Juan, like his friends, began to experiment with different types of drugs, enjoying the way they made him feel so powerful and carefree.

Juan also spent many hours playing video games. He was very good at it, and could make a few pesos last for hours. Often he would not arrive home until well after midnight.

During this time, Juan was exposed to all kinds of dangers, but for the most part it seemed that God had His hand on him, protecting him from really serious harm. Even so, the problems at home continued to grow, hence Juan was spending more and more time away from home, slipping ever so slowly toward perdition.

CHAPTER FIFTEEN

* * *

I Surrender

* * *

He who cannot forgive breaks the bridge over which
he himself must pass.

–George Herbert

As I was in the midst of thinking about what to do with AdaptaSoft, I was reminded of an earlier time in my life when I had also needed to surrender. It had been about eight years earlier, when I was facing another crisis in my life.

I was in college at the time, and had gone to one of my favorite places on campus--the top of the Wood Street parking garage. It was a place that I had discovered one night while jogging, and I had returned there occasionally to pray, or just reflect.

From the top of the garage I could look out over the entire Lafayette area, and on this particular night, the weather was perfect, with lights gleaming far into the distance. I went there struggling with rejection and confusion, having arrived at my breaking point. I knew I had to surrender, or else I would end up going nuts.

Until I was 23, I had never given any thought to getting married. But once I started, I couldn't think about anything else--and when I thought about who to marry, I couldn't think about anyone other than Joy.

I prayed about it, and felt led to propose--but when I did, Joy said "no." I had been so sure that she was the one for me, and had carefully thought and planned everything out. I even had 41 Bible verses to prove it. When she said "no," I was devastated.

My whole faith was tested, and I fretted, prayed, and worried for months. Finally I arrived at the top of the garage.

It was strange. Although I felt completely alone, I sensed God telling me to let Him carry this burden. Eventually, through my tears, I prayed out loud, "Lord, I can't carry this anymore. If I don't marry Joy, it's OK. Whatever you want for me is OK with me."

At that moment, I was able to surrender the very thing that I felt was God's will for my life. I decided to be content with whatever He had planned for me--no matter what I thought. With that surrender came the most incredible feeling of freedom. For the first time in months, I had peace.

The amazing thing was that not long after that rooftop moment, Joy changed her mind--or rather, came to her senses! But this only happened after I had completely surrendered my will to God.

Eight years later, while recalling this particular time in my life, I realized that there was something else I needed to surrender--and that was the anger I had for Dakota. It was time to forgive them. The reality was that this grudge was doing more harm to me than it was to them. My obsession for justice was also destroying AdaptaSoft and the morale of my employees.

I started to pray about it, and I also started to pray for the individuals who had personally caused me so much pain. I tried to put myself in their shoes, and as I did, I began to understand how losing their main customer would have been devastating. I also realized that even though it was not our fault, Dakota would naturally have wanted to blame someone else. We just happened to be an easy target. I even saw areas where we, in our eagerness, may have been at fault too, and I was willing to accept that.

As I prayed for these individuals, my anger and hatred began to seep away, and I felt a great burden lift from my shoulders. I had a peace about becoming reconciled to them, and so began to pray for that reconciliation between our two companies.

This reconciliation was exactly what my employees wanted, and was a key ingredient in the sale of the company. They wanted to do whatever was needed in order to resolve the dispute peacefully. Eventually they did settle the dispute out of court, agreeing to pay Dakota a sum of money over time. As it turned out, the agreed figure was exactly the amount that we had thought it would be early in the proceedings. If I had agreed to pay that in the beginning, it would have saved everyone a lot of grief--not to mention the quite substantial attorney fees.

But that was all still in the future. At this point, I was finally sure that I needed to completely surrender my company. I still didn't want to look like a quitter, but knew that it didn't really matter how I looked.

The company was ready for a new stage of its development, and it was a good time for me to step out. I was impressed by the courage of the young men who had taken the risk of making me an offer, and I decided to trust them. That was when I completely surrendered, and as soon as I did, there came an immediate sense of peace.

My employees were excited to hear that I had changed my mind, but it took a while for us to work out the details of the sale. The agreement we arrived at was a far cry from what they had first offered, but it didn't matter.

Soon I was unemployed, and without a clue as to what I would do next. Joy and I both felt that God was leading us to get involved in some type of ministry, but we didn't know what. All I knew was that I had finally found peace. As for our future, we had a simple faith that God would direct us and reveal His plans, in His perfect time.

CHAPTER SIXTEEN

* * *

Waiting on the Lord

* * *

I believe in the tragic element of history.
I believe there is the tragedy of a man
who works very hard and never gets what he wants.
And then I believe there is the even more bitter tragedy
of a man who finally gets what he wants
and finds out that he doesn't want it.

–Henry Kissinger

For a month after I sold AdaptaSoft, we were very happy. My former employees who took over management of Adaptasoft did some things that could have offended me--such as changing the locks on the company doors and making me sign an unnecessarily restrictive, non-compete contract—but it didn't really bother me. It was a big change for everyone, and I figured they were just trying to be businesslike and thorough. Joy and I felt at peace knowing that we were doing God's will, and I was just thankful to be moving on to another chapter in our lives.

Even though I was unemployed, I was still staying busy. I had some "to-do" jobs around the house to finish up, but basically just wanted to spend lots of time with my family. I took up jogging outside when I could, or rode the Nordic-track when the weather was bad. Before long, I began to lose weight and get into better shape.

Losing the extra pounds I had carried, I felt so much better physically, and spiritually I felt better too. It was a special, peaceful time of waiting on the Lord to direct us, and it was a new feeling to be so open and surrendered to whatever He had in store. I really didn't have any good ideas as to what that direction may be, although I did think about writing a book. In fact, I even gave it a try, but found it very difficult. In the end I decided that I must not have that particular gift.

For that first month, I wasn't at all anxious about the future. However, after that month had passed and my household "to-do" list was done, I found myself becoming a little antsy. By then, I had realized that I wouldn't make it as an author, and I definitely wasn't interested in starting another business.

In the fall of 2000, we started working with the Purdue group on the Bible distribution program that a good friend had started. During that time, we had the idea of adding a website called www. FreeBibleNow.org. We were trying to reach out to others, doing some counseling and visiting, but we knew that we still hadn't found what God wanted us to do.

I didn't doubt that God would eventually show us what we were to do, and still had a peace about it, but I was getting restless and growing tired of being around the house all the time. I felt like saying, "Here I am Lord; send me."

Unfortunately, by then, the relationship with my previous employees at Adaptasoft and I was deteriorating. Small disputes slowly eroded trust. I was beginning to have doubts as to whether they were really committed to upholding their end of the sale agreement. I had left them all the assets, including the cash and accounts receivable. This was a very unusual arrangement, but I knew that they would need the money to cash flow the business. Obviously, I wanted them to be successful ... but the doubts haunted me.

I began to worry that they might end up not paying me anything at all and still leave me with the company's liabilities. I was far more concerned about the latter, than the former. I had heard of people selling their companies, and then actually losing money, rather than gaining. I didn't want that to happen, but there wasn't anything I could do. Once the business was sold, I had no control over what they did at AdaptaSoft.

Another month went by, and then one morning, a new direction opened.

We were still in bed when the telephone rang, and after answering it, Joy handed the receiver to me and whispered, "It's for you."

"Who is it?" I whispered back, but Joy only shrugged.

Covering the mouthpiece, I practiced saying "good morning" a few times, to try and work the morning cobwebs out of my voice. Then I removed my hand, and finally said, "Good morning!"

My voice still cracked.

"Good morning, Bob," the voice on the other end replied. "This is Barry Bahler calling from FBi Buildings. Hope I didn't call too early."

"No, No, you're fine. It's good to hear from you."

And it was. After two months of unemployment, I was really ready to do something--but didn't know exactly what.

Barry was the CEO of FBi Buildings, a local construction company, and his call that morning was to inform me that they were looking for a new manager of their computer department. He wanted to know if I would be interested in applying.

I was flattered that they had thought of me. I also wondered how they knew of me, and that I was unemployed.

I told Barry that I was available, but hadn't actually been looking for work. Then I was about to tell him that I was not interested, when something told me not to turn them down outright. Perhaps it was the pleasant conversation that I had with the CEO, who was a very warm and understanding gentleman.

"I will definitely pray about it and let you know if I am interested," I promised.

At first, the idea of going back to work didn't interest me. I had thought that we were supposed to dedicate ourselves to some type of mission work, and this job offer didn't sound like what God had planned. However, because I was having doubts about the sale of AdaptaSoft, I realized that having a job and paycheck was really a sensible thing to do.

It may seem strange, but after having been my own boss for so long, the thought of working for someone else actually sounded really attractive to me. I had also heard wonderful things about FBi and couldn't think of a better company to work for.

As Joy and I prayed about interviewing for the job, I had immediate peace about it and called the CEO back on the same day. I had a great deal of respect for this company and the people that worked there, and I sensed that the Lord was working in and through them.

During the interviews that followed, I was open and frank about my belief that God was calling our family to the mission field, but admitted that I didn't, as yet, know how or what that would entail.

I have no doubt that it was God's will that I work for this company, because they still offered me the job.

I started working at FBi in December 2000, and remained with them for almost two years. I honestly cannot say enough good about that company. They were all wonderful people--from the CEO to the cleaning lady.

When I left, at the end of 2002, it was with the hope that I had been able to do something to help them during my time there. I feel like they blessed me way more than I deserved--and more than I was able to bless them in return.

CHAPTER SEVENTEEN

* * *

Going to Mexico?!

* * *

Real joy comes not from ease or riches
or from the praise of men,
but from doing something worthwhile.

–Wilfred T. Grenfell

About six months after I started at FBi, one of the managers asked me to join the communications committee of World Relief, which is the humanitarian arm of our church.

I had looked up to this man since the days when I had been a young Christian and he a mature leader in the church youth group. I jumped at the chance to work with him and get involved in the committee, even though I had no idea what I would be doing for them.

At our first meeting, they dropped the bombshell. They wanted someone to go to Mexico and take pictures of the church's construction project at an orphanage. The pictures were to be used for slide presentations for the churches that were supporting the work.

Then they said, "Bob, we all think this would be a great first assignment for you."

"Mee-ee?" my voice creaked.

I got a big lump in my throat at the thought of going to Mexico--I literally could not swallow for a few seconds! The thought of leaving the country scared me to death. In fact, my hands began to sweat at the thought of going somewhere where you couldn't even drink the water!

I had never been to Mexico, and for good reason. To be honest, I had even been scared when we traveled to Canada. We couldn't even go camping because I just couldn't be without a bathroom.

The bathroom fear stemmed from a trauma I suffered as a child in a public restroom. Some teenage boys had opened the door to the stall I was using and taunted me. I was a shy child, and the humilia-tion affected me. After that, I found it difficult to use any bathroom other than the ones at home. For that reason, I didn't like traveling at all, let alone to a third world country!

Once, when we were visiting Joy's sister in Southern California, the suggestion was made that we jump into Tijuana Mexico for a few hours. I told Joy that I didn't want to go and had no confidence, whatsoever, in that country. But she insisted it would be safe. After all, so many people visit there--what could possibly go wrong?

During the short drive to the border, we heard an emergency news bulletin on the radio. Colosio, the PRI candidate for President of Mexico, had been assassinated in Tijuana, of all places.

After hearing that, I told everyone we were not going to Mexico that day! We turned around and went to the beach instead.

[Note: It turns out that Colosio, who would have been president of Mexico had he not been killed by a faction of his own party, was from Magdalena, where we later started an orphanage.]

All these memories were running through my mind as I sat in that first committee meeting. No one thought to ask me if I was OK with the idea of going to Mexico. Instead, they all thought it was a fantastic plan, and took my terrified silence as acceptance. To be honest, I was too busy trying to sort through my fears to be able to formulate any sort of reasonable refusal.

I was to go as part of a work team during the first week of January 2002, so I took some comfort from the fact that I would have a little time to mentally prepare myself. The only other work team I had been on was to Alabama when I was 16--and I nearly died on that trip! We had worked three days in the rain, and by the time we headed for home, I was really sick with very bad diarrhea and cramps. The bumpy, nine hour, van ride home was pure torture. After that experi-ence, I had vowed I would never go on a work team again--but here I was being volunteered to do just that. I figured if I almost died from sickness in Alabama, I would never survive Mexico!

I had never had life insurance before, mainly because I didn't really believe in it. But with the trip to Mexico looming, I had second thoughts. In fact, I was so worried that I may not come back from the trip, that I took out a term policy. When I calculated my chances for survival, life insurance looked like too good a deal to pass up.

Even though I was generally terrified about leaving the safety of the US, for some reason I never refused to go to Mexico--I just knew I had to go. It was a small miracle, but I felt a strange peace knowing that God was either going to protect me and see me through, or else take me home to be with Him. I sensed that this trip was somehow part of His plan for us.

I remember kissing Joy and the girls goodbye, soaking in the last glimpse of each one as if I would never see them again. Salome, with her beautiful brown eyes, chubby cheeks, and cheerful personality. Chloe, with her sparkling blue eyes, slender frame and spunky personality. Joy, supporting me with her loving, 'I'm going to miss you' smile. I would not let myself cry, even though I felt like it. I wanted them to remember me as being happy, in case this was the last time they ever saw me.

I was taking great comfort in the fact that two other brothers from my home church were also going on the trip. I was determined to stick close by them--preferably slightly behind them.

As I made my preparations to go to the orphanage in Imuris, Mexico, Juan was getting ready to go there too.

CHAPTER EIGHTEEN

* * *

Casa de Elizabeth

* * *

Those who wish to sing, always find a song.

- Swedish proverb

When Juan turned 12, he told his mother that he had decided to leave home for good and live on the street with the friends he had made there. He was ready to leave all his family behind and go out on his own.

Sara was heartbroken. Even though she hadn't been able to raise her son, or provide for him as she would have liked, she still loved him and wanted him to have the opportunity of having a better life than her own. She really believed that Juan was special and could not stand the thought of him living on the street at such a young age--particularly with all the drugs and violence.

This concern, together with Juan's bouts of anger and depression, caused Sara to finally seek help from DIF, the social services office, in late 2001. They recommended that she send Juan to an orphanage, where he could have the opportunity to return to school and start fresh.

When Sara shared the idea with Juan, he didn't hesitate. It was just the change he was looking for. In fact, he was so excited that he could hardly wait to go.

It was hard for Sara to let him go, but in her heart she knew she had already lost him. She didn't want her son to be a drunk, or a drug addict, or grow old in jail. She *didn't* want him to be like his father, and the orphanage seemed to be her only hope of saving him.

She had heard of other children that had been helped at orphanages, and this encouraged her. Sara knew that this particular orphanage was close to the border and received many American visitors who provided help for the children. Her prayer was that Juan's life would be turned around, and she had a strange premonition that he was going to meet an American at the orphanage, who would help him.

Eventually the day arrived for Juan's trip to the orphanage. He wasn't the only boy going, and the DIF car had to make several stops in order to pick up other children. Juan was excited to see his new home.

Finally they were at the last stop, but not all the children were as excited to go as Juan. When the driver got out at the last house, two boys slipped out of the car and ran away. Juan didn't realize what had happened until the driver returned. Much to Juan's disappointment, the trip had to be postponed until the runaways could be found.

A couple of days later they were ready to try again. There were several children packed into the back seat of a small pickup. There was a boy named Hector, who was the older brother of one of Juan's old school friends. Another was an absolutely beautiful girl, named Elizabeth, who was the same age as him.

Juan had never met Elizabeth before, and got to know her during the nine hour trip from Navojoa to Imuris. It was cold outside and turbulent wind carried a chill, so Elizabeth and Juan cuddled together under a blanket. In the privacy of that blanket cover, the two kissed for the first time. They felt camaraderie, and a special friendship began that would continue for the time they were both at the orphanage.

Finally they pulled into the Casa de Elizabeth Orphanage. CE is built on a mesa overlooking a green, river valley, surrounded by breathtakingly beautiful mountains. Every day the light paints the mountains in different colors.

There were about 100 children in the orphanage, ranging in age from 3 to 18 years old. Together with the other children, Juan stepped out of the car and began to get to know his new world. It was October 27, 2001, and Juan was just days away from his 13th birthday.

At first, Juan was intimidated by all the new faces, rules, and procedures. Most of the other children ignored him--they were used to seeing children come and go.

He liked the flush toilets in the bathroom, but thought that it would have been nice if there had been partitions to offer some privacy. He didn't mind that the room was filthy and musty, but he wasn't used to bathing--let alone with so many others. Juan was used to more privacy, and so was careful to pick a shower that still had a curtain. Even then, he showered in his underwear.

There was a big room, stuffed with clothes from floor to ceiling, where a kind woman gave him a set of clothes to wear every day after he showered. Juan was thrilled to be clean and have new clothes, socks, underwear, and shoes.

Meals were served in a large cafeteria, and a child was always asked to say a prayer before everyone started eating. They mostly ate oatmeal, beans, rice, potatoes and eggs. Sometimes they would have a meal bone soup.

Juan immediately started back at school, and felt a new motivation from being with other children that had similar problems. He dedicated himself to study, and to trying to get good grades.

About two weeks after Juan arrived at CE, he celebrated his 13th birthday by eating pizza for the first time in his life. He had always wanted to eat pizza, so when one of the orphanage counselors asked him what he wanted to eat on his birthday, he didn't hesitate.

Eating pizza was a high point for Juan ... but it was downhill from there. The newness and allure of the orphanage began to wear off, and he grew tired of cold beans and rice. There was constant fighting between the boys, and the older, bigger boys beat up on the smaller boys. Juan had been in several fights already and had taken some beatings. There was an established hierarchy, and the ones above you took whatever they wanted. Juan had nothing--his shoes, toothpaste, clothes, even his school books, were stolen. It was impossible to keep anything of even the smallest value. Even if you had a locker with a padlock, someone would break it open and steal whatever was inside.

Christmas at the orphanage was a time when everyone stayed up late and ate junk food. There were hundreds of visitors to Casa de Elizabeth--many Mexicans, but far more Americans. They brought hot dogs, hamburgers, and tons of gifts. Juan was delighted with the food, but the toys were soon stolen and broken.

It was a crazy time, as the children went wild after eating ridiculous amounts of candy, junk food, and pop. They fought over toys, got sick from eating too many sweets, and generally behaved badly.

After the visitors left, all was quiet. School had not yet resumed, and Juan was bored. With nothing to distract him, he started to think about his past and felt sad.

Then, on that stormy night in the desert, Juan reached his lowest point and physically cried out to God for help. He was discouraged and ready to give up, until he heard that another group of Americans were coming to visit the first week of January. It was a spark of hope--something he and the others looked forward to.

CHAPTER NINETEEN

* * *

South of the Border

* * *

Do not go where the path may lead,
go instead where there is no path and leave a trail.

- Ralph Waldo Emerson

I was nervous enough about crossing the border into Mexico without having to drive one of the vehicles as well--but that's exactly what they wanted me to do! My original plan had been to hide in the back seat, where I would have more time for prayer. Then I found out that I was expected to drive. I wanted to refuse, but that would have meant admitting how scared I was, so I didn't.

To make matters more interesting, we went in at night. As soon as we crossed the border, it got very dark, and I was left to wonder where all the streetlights had gone.

Then, much to our distress, the lead vehicle took a wrong turn. So instead of using the bypass that would have avoided all the traffic and congestion, we had to cross through downtown Nogales.

As if that wasn't enough, we had picked the worse day of the year for that particular trip! It was December 31, 2001--New Years Eve. Downtown Nogales was a circus! There were people everywhere-- prostitutes, fire breathers, soldiers with machine guns, vendors, and beggars.

Suddenly, armed men in dark uniforms were motioning for me to pull over. The other vehicles had gone ahead, and I had to stop alone. It turned out to be a routine border check. Our car had gotten a "red light," which meant I should have stopped, but I had no clue what was going on.

I was flabbergasted when an angry-looking Mexican man started yelling at me. Not knowing what to do, I quickly locked the car doors, and then opened the window a crack. Not understanding any Spanish at all, I had no idea what the inspector was saying, and by this point, was getting quite panicky. In fact, I seriously started to think about making a run back toward the US border.

Finally, I opened the door and got out. The man was still talking gibberish to me and making hand signals, but I wasn't looking at him. I was looking at the border, which I could still see from where I was standing--clean streets, lights, and a very inviting McDonalds' sign. I figured if I ran in a zigzag pattern, they probably wouldn't be able to shoot me down. I wanted so bad to be back in the good ol' US of A! Everything in me said, "Run!"

My heart was pounding, but I tried to tell myself not to panic. I could still see the other vehicles in our caravan, which by then had noticed that we had been pulled over. They had stopped to wait just up the street--causing a small traffic jam in the process. People began to stare at me, perhaps seeing the raw terror on my face.

I was about to make a run for the US, when I thought of them calling Joy and saying,

"Uh, Joy, I don't know how to tell you this, but Bob never made it to Mexico. He, well uh, he chickened ... I mean ... he froze up at the border and took off running. He left the car running, and the rest of us sitting there. We're not sure where he is now. The police are out looking for him…."

As that scenario played out in my mind, I came to my senses. I knew if I did that, it would be something that I would regret my entire life. I felt ashamed, and decided that I had to confront this fear.

Finally I understood that the man was saying "oh-PAYN, oh-PAYN," or "open," in English. I realized that they wanted to look at the luggage in the trunk, so I quickly began putting the bags up on the tables for inspection.

I had them all there in short order, but it turned out that they only looked in a few bags, and we were soon on our way again.

I breathed a huge sigh of relief and felt myself quickly bonding with the other passengers in the car. I thought that this must be what it is like for soldiers in combat. We were all in it together--brave, strong men, who were willing to lay down our lives for one another, and never turning our backs! No! And definitely not running when the going got tough!

Our rental car was a black Mercury Marci. We thought it looked suspiciously like a mafia car, which is probably why they stopped us at the border. So we dubbed the car, "The Mafia Mobile."

We managed to make it through downtown Nogales without falling into any of the huge potholes, or holes dug by work crews. These holes were sometimes so big that a whole car could drop right in, and the only warning that they were there was usually a single, unlit cone. Huge metal I-beams would rise in the middle of the road, without so much as a single barrel or guard rail. There was no shoulder on most of the road--just a six-inch drop-off.

The difference was striking, but all of a sudden I found myself enjoying the excitement, and for the first time, was starting to forget my fears. It was the beginning of what was to be an experience that would change my life forever.

CHAPTER TWENTY

* * *

A Life Changing Experience

* * *

Besides the noble art of getting things done,
there is the noble art of leaving things undone.
The wisdom of life consists in
the elimination of nonessentials.

–Lin Yutang

With great anticipation, I took in each new sight as we rounded one curve after another.

It had been dark when we arrived at the hotel the night before, so we hadn't been able to see much. However, the light of morning revealed shocking scenes of poverty. I had never, personally, seen living conditions so poor before, and couldn't understand how anyone could actually live in the cardboard and tin shacks we saw. Some homes were made out of wooden pallets, others only had three walls. These shacks went on for miles--as far as I could see. Smoke from small cooking fires, and dust from dirt roads, created a haze that seemed to obscure the whole region.

We survived the night in the hotel, amidst the sound of small-arms fire and traffic noise. I had slept fairly well, which wasn't surprising, as I was beyond exhausted.

Excited to see more of Mexico, I awoke before daybreak and headed out for a short walk. As I went, I was startled by a group of tough-looking soldiers--"Federales" as they were called--who were camped out behind our hotel. Evidently, they were there to protect us, and I didn't know whether to be comforted by that, or disturbed to know that they thought it was necessary to guard us from harm.

On Monday morning, we continued on our way to the orphanage. We drove slowly through the small town of Imuris, past the small plaza and the Catholic Church, down a steep hill, across a railroad track and over a long bridge. The main street was lined with small shops made of thick, adobe brick. Every window was protected by steel bars. All the streets were deserted, as it was New Years Day.

The pothole-filled road curved back and forth. When we turned off onto a dirt road, I sensed we were getting close. The car groaned as we swayed and bounced over the uneven surface. Then the road narrowed and turned into bumpy stones. Finally we pulled into the long driveway of Casa de Elizabeth.

I was immediately enchanted by the orphanage. The buildings were of crude construction, yet their plateau setting provided a breathtaking view of a mountainous valley.

As soon as we parked, sleepy-eyed children surrounded our vehicles. They were jabbering excitedly, and I couldn't understand a word.

There were so many children, and every one of them seemed beautiful to me. I asked myself, "Why wouldn't someone want these children?" They were all so friendly, and I immediately found myself wishing I could talk to them, or at least have a better way of communicating with them. They showered us with love, and I desperately wanted to do something for them in return.

That week, I divided my time between construction work and taking pictures--something I did for a couple of hours every day. During that time, I took hundreds of photos of both the construction and the children.

The children seemed to like having their pictures taken, but there was a problem--they just stared at the camera with blank faces. This was disappointing, because they were so beautiful when they smiled. But I didn't know how to encourage them to do that, and I didn't want them to look sad in the pictures.

I asked my companions if anyone knew how to say the word "smile" in Spanish, but no one did. Then I remembered that "Feliz Navidad" meant "Merry Christmas," so decided to try saying "feliz." It worked great! The children smiled widely, and I was thrilled that I could communicate a little bit!

I was able to get almost all the children to smile that day, but there was one child who wouldn't. I had tried twice to take a picture of him, but both times he just looked at me with the same sad eyes.

Noticing the blue Chicago Cubs jacket he was wearing, I had the urge to tell him I had seen a Cubs game once at Wrigley field when I worked my internship there--but, of course, I had no way of communicating that. I simply pointed to the jacket and made motions of swinging a baseball bat. I smiled widely. Juan nodded, but without a hint of a smile. Although I didn't think too long about it at the time, it bothered me. There was an emptiness in his eyes.

While taking photos again the next day, I found the same boy playing marbles in the dirt, and learned that his name was Juan. I was intrigued by the children's incredible accuracy--hitting the other marbles from several feet away.

As I was watching Juan and another boy play, Juan motioned an invitation to me, and then placed several marbles in my hand. I was touched that he would offer to show me how to play, and so I tried. Of course, I soon found out that I was losing all Juan's marbles, as I had no accuracy at all. I had never played the game before.

I wanted to continue playing with them, but didn't have any more marbles to lose. Without thinking, I pulled out a dollar and offered to buy some marbles from them. Instantly, they both wanted to sell their marbles--but I only had one dollar. Jose, the younger, more forward boy, made the sale, leaving both Juan and me feeling bad.

Juan was noticeably saddened that he had not earned the dollar, and I was devastated too. Here was a boy who wouldn't smile, and all I had done was discourage him further! I felt like whipping out a 20 dollar bill and stuffing it into his hand--but I knew I shouldn't. I tried to tell him I was sorry. He just looked at me with the same sad expression and shrugged his shoulders, as if to say that it was all right.

Then, with great patience, he continued to show me how to play marbles. I soon lost all the marbles I had purchased, which turned out to be a good business deal for Jose! Yet, even though the game came to an end, it was the start of a new friendship that would, ultimately, change our lives.

The week went by so fast, and when it came time to go, I could hardly bear to think of leaving. I didn't want to leave such a special place. I had made a few friends among the wonderful children, and the thought of not seeing them again was more than I could bear. We were taking pictures and giving goodbye hugs, when a few of the brothers started to give their tools to some of the boys. I took a picture of the children lined up with their tool belts, hammers, and tape measures. They were so proud, but Juan did not yet have any tools.

Despite my best efforts, Juan still didn't smile for the picture. I had tried every day to get him to smile, without much success. I perceived that this boy was hurting, and I desperately wanted to do something for him--but I didn't know what I could do. Then an idea struck.

After the photo was taken, I motioned to Juan to follow me around to the trunk of our car. Opening my suitcase, I started giving him my tools, and for the first time I saw him really smile--a big, beautiful smile. Juan looked as though he was going to cry for joy. "Tank you!" he said, repeatedly, after each tool was handed to him.

I didn't know what he would do with them, but I gave him every-thing I had--except for the utility knife!

I had been so impressed with all the children, but Juan had been especially kind that week, offering me his place in the candy line, and so forth. Before we left, I asked someone to snap a picture of Juan and me together.

When I had to say goodbye to Juan, I could see that he was very sad. He repeatedly said, "No tomorrow?" Then he asked if I would come again.

Although I didn't understand his words, I could easily under-stand his expressions and gestures. I had no way of sharing my heart with him, or showing any of these dear children what they meant to me. Instead, I had to turn my back on them and walk away. It was one of the most heart-wrenching things I have ever done. I could only wave goodbye as we drove away.

It was an emotional time, and I found it difficult to sort out why I felt the way I did. I wanted to cry, but I couldn't even do that. All I knew was that something important had happened, and I could not wait to return to the orphanage. I had to go back!

CHAPTER TWENTY-ONE

* * *

Back Home

* * *

The only thing worse than a husband who never notices
what you cook or what you wear, is a husband who
always notices what you cook and what you wear.

–Sandra Litoff

"Did you miss us?" Joy asked.

"Not until I was on my way home," I admitted.

"But you did think of us while you were away, didn't you?" Joy looked worried.

I paused for a second, then confessed, "Well, not really."

Immediately I realized that I had said the wrong thing.

"Bob! That's terrible!" Joy exclaimed, punching me playfully in the arm, but sounding genuinely hurt.

"I'm sorry. I don't mean it like that," I explained. "It's just that it was like I was in a totally--*totally*--different world down there. I was so overwhelmed by the experience that I forgot all about everything back here."

"Hmmph!" My wife was not impressed.

"But I missed you so much as soon as we started home," I tried to recover, taking Joy in my arms.

"Well I missed you, and prayed for you, the *whole* time," Joy said, still sounding disgruntled, and offering only half a smile.

I was happy to be reunited with my family and loved ones, but I was also frustrated because I didn't know how to explain the way I felt. All I could think about were those beautiful, fatherless children and how they had been content with so very little. I had hardly invested anything, yet felt so blessed to be able to give them a little joy through the gift of a few tools. I had made huge returns on financial investments in the past, but never had I received such a large return on such a small investment.

Our big house didn't love us back. It was beautiful, and I was able to take some satisfaction in a good outcome--but really, who did it all benefit? It had never been the same without Dad, and I knew in my heart that it really meant nothing.

On the other hand, there were hurting children out there--and that did mean something to me.

I also couldn't stop thinking of Jesus' words in Matthew 6:19-20, that we are not to store up treasures on earth, but rather to store up treasures in heaven instead. I no longer had any interest in any of the financial empires on earth. I wanted to do something that had eternal value.

That first night home, as Joy and I lay in bed in the darkness, I told her something that I would not have dared mention to anyone else at the time.

"Joy?" I whispered. She made a noise. "Are you awake?"

"Yeah," she said sleepily.

"Oh, sorry honey. I didn't want to wake you," I said, then paused.

"What is it?" Joy asked.

"Oh, nothing really. I'll tell you later." Now I hesitated to say what was on my heart.

"Well I'm wide awake now, so you might as well tell me."

"Uh ... it's just I don't really know how to say it," I said.

"Just tell me," she said, taking me in her arms. "You know I'll understand."

"OK," I sighed deeply. "I think God might be calling us to go to Mexico."

* * *

Later that week, as I was going through the hundreds of pictures I had taken while in Mexico, I was stopped by the first photo of Juan.

Once again, I was bothered by the fact that he would not smile. There he was, looking at me with his dark, diamond-shaped eyes.

They say that the eye is a window to the soul, and when I peered into Juan's window, something about his expression called out to me for help. I sensed God was saying, "Help this child." I didn't know what that meant, but I couldn't shake the feeling.

Of course, at the time I didn't know that Juan's mother had sent him to this specific orphanage on the border of the US, with the hope and prayer that an American would visit and help him. I also didn't know just how much Juan was hurting, or that he had been literally crying out to God for help.

We already sponsored children in Haiti--children that we had never met. So I asked Joy if she would be interested in sponsoring a child in Mexico as well. She agreed, and I immediately made a phone call to find out where to send the money.

During that telephone conversation, I asked if, by chance, we would be able to sponsor a boy called Juan, who was 13 years old. The woman on the other end of the line said that she thought she had heard of this particular child. In fact, she thought that he may have just arrived and promised to check on it and let us know. As it turned out, it was Juan, and as he didn't have a sponsor, he was assigned to us.

With joy in my heart, I lovingly made a care package for Juan and several of the other children that I had met at CE. The box was filled with things like chocolate, pictures, notes, and clothes. I also wrote a note for each child. Juan's note said how glad we were to be able to sponsor him. Using translating software, I was able to tell him in Spanish that we were praying for him. As a final thought, I included the picture of him and me. Then I sealed the box and shipped it off to the orphanage.

I wanted desperately to do something to help those children. It didn't matter if it was big or small. I was trying to find any excuse to go back to Imuris, and I didn't have to look too hard.

I had previously talked to the orphanage director about helping them with a five-year plan, and it was this plan that I used as my excuse to return to Mexico. But before I went, I crammed for four weeks straight, several hours a day, learning Spanish. I read Spanish, listened to it on the radio, and talked to anyone who spoke it. It was amazing how fast I was picking it up. By the time my second trip arrived, I could actually speak a little of the language.

In the meantime, Juan and the other boys had received the gifts. The clothes were put in the bodega, and the food quickly devoured, but Juan was curious about this American who had cared enough to think of him. He carefully put the picture I had sent in his wallet.

* * *

A Letter from Juan to his Mother...

Dear Mom, I am fine. I miss you. I want you to know that I am sorry for all the problems that we had. It was my fault. I love you, Juan.

PS: I have an American friend.

CHAPTER TWENTY-TWO

* * *

The Second Trip

* * *

But whoso hath this world's good,
and seeth his brother have need,
and shutteth up his bowels of compassion from him,
how dwelleth the love of God in him?

I John 3:17

It was late February when we arrived at Casa de Elizabeth the second time. Jerry was the World Relief coordinator for the Imuris project, and had been our guide for my first trip to Mexico. He made regular trips down from Phoenix to Mexico, so I had been able to catch a ride down with him for my second visit. We had been spending some time together, and were becoming fast friends.

When Jerry and I arrived at the orphanage, a group of boys ran over to the pickup. I was surprised that they remembered us. My heart was pounding with the excitement of being back, and I was thrilled to see all the children again. Before long, I was busy giving hugs and pats on the back.

Juan gave me a big hug and a huge smile, which touched my heart. Then he took out his wallet and showed me the picture I had sent of the two of us. I was so glad to see him and anxious to learn more about this boy we had chosen to sponsor.

Because Jerry spoke Spanish, I asked him to help me speak to Juan. Through Jerry, I asked him a little about his family and past, but I quickly sensed that my questions were far too personal, and therefore changed the subject. I understood very little and felt bad for even trying to find out.

While at the orphanage that week, I roomed with Ricardo, a missionary who was staying at CE for a time and had turned a storage room into his living quarters. The room was a chaotic mess--stacked from floor to ceiling with junk, and bags of clothing that had apparently been donated to the orphanage. Rick was a Vietnam veteran and still had some of his military gear with him, which added to the cornucopia of other items laying everywhere.

As I was just getting to know Rick, he made a point of showing me his military knife. It had a long, heavy, razor-sharp blade, and looked like it could easily dismember a body in a hurry. I didn't know Rick at the time, or his slightly unconventional personality, so my first thought was that he was plain nuts, and that I was going to be spending the week with a crazy ex-soldier with a very deadly weapon.

However, as I visited with Rick more, I began to feel at ease. We soon got to know one another, and I slept better at night. But I did always try to make sure Rick was in a good mood before we went to sleep--just to be on the safe side!

One night after we turned out the lights, I shared with Rick what was on my heart.

"Rick?"

"What's up, bro?" he replied.

"Just checking to see if you were asleep," I said.

"Nope, just saying my prayers. I usually pray myself to sleep."

"Well, I don't want to interrupt."

"Not at all, if something's on your mind, spit it out."

"OK, well..." I began, "I know it seems ridiculous, but I sometimes feel God is calling us to Mexico."

It was the first time I had shared it with anyone other than Joy.

"Bob, that's fantastic!" Rick responded enthusiastically.

"Well, it just seems so weird. I mean we have a house, our families, church, my job. And to pick up and move, I...."

"Whoa-whoa-whoa! Hold your horses, bro. This sounds like something we need to commit to prayer right now," he insisted.

"Right now?" I asked.

Rick answered my question when I saw him out of bed and already kneeling. I joined him in prayer on the cold, hard, concrete floor. He put a firm hand on my shoulder and began to pray.

"Lord, we come to you this night with the request for Bob that you will reveal your will for him and his family. Bob is willing, Lord, to serve you. We ask that if it's your will, that you will give him a sign; that you will demonstrate your power and your love for him. And that you will demonstrate your love for these dear children here in Imuris, and all over Mexico, and the poverty stricken nations of the world. We praise you, Lord, as we know that you are worthy and will do more than we ask. In the precious name of Jesus, our Lord and Savior. Amen!"

"Amen!" I said, wiping a tear from my cheek. Then added, "Thank you Rick. I feel a peace about it now."

"Don't mention it, bro. Sleep good.

"You too. Hasta mañana."

"Hasta mañana."

* * *

The next day, during the mid-week church service at the orphanage, God touched my heart. It wasn't a final answer, but it was something special. I was sitting with the children when we sang "The Old Rugged Cross" in Spanish. I didn't understand all the words in Spanish, but I knew them in English. My heart was touched by the singing and the surroundings--I wept through the whole song.

I still wasn't sure what it meant, but I sensed that there was something significant about the event. I shared the experience with Rick, and he encouraged me to keep praying.

"I am completely confident that God will reveal His will," he said. "It's strange, but I have a feeling that you're being called. Just remember to be flexible. Things don't always go as we plan."

During that week, I did the necessary research in order to complete the five-year plan, but for the most part, I hung out with Richard and the children, and worked on improving my limited Spanish. Although I was still struggling, it was a thrill to be able to communicate--I had learned so much in a short time.

One day they asked me to go to a local store to buy milk for a baby. I couldn't begin to understand their directions, so asked Juan to go with me. As we walked to the store, I started a conversation.

"Juan, what is your house like?" I asked, in my broken Spanish.

"I don't understand," Juan replied. It was a common response in those early days when we were still learning how to communicate. Thankfully he was patient.

"In your hometown, what was your house like?" I tried again.

"It is small...."

Although Juan said more, I didn't understand it.

"Was it like that house?" I asked, pointing to a small, brick building."

"No."

"Was it like that one? This time I pointed to an unpainted, block house."

"No."

My Spanish was improving, but I still didn't understand the words he was using to describe his house. Then he pointed to a small shack made out of scrap wood and black tarpaper.

"It's like that one," he said, matter-of-factly.

I couldn't believe that Juan had come from such a meager existence. The shack didn't look good enough for an animal, let along a human. The question of how he had survived was more than I could comprehend. I had only been trying to understand a little more about his past, but felt bad for asking. I quickly changed the subject.

* * *

On the last day of my visit, I walked with some of the boys to school. We arrived early, so I sat with Juan at the edge of the basketball court. Usually he had something to say, but this time he sat with his face in his hands, strangely silent.

"Are you sad?" I asked. Juan did not respond.

"What's wrong?" I pried, half knowing what he was feeling. I was feeling it too.

"Tomorrow you are going to leave..." he managed, before breaking up. My heart sank as tears started coursing down his cheeks. A lump grew in my throat, and I began crying too.

The little guy had stolen my heart. I didn't know his past and I didn't know why he was in an orphanage. All I knew was that he seemed like a very special young man. Juan had learned to play the guitar and would sing beautiful Christian songs. I couldn't imagine why his parents would not want him.

In an effort to comfort him, I put my hand on his shoulder. I didn't know what to say. For whatever reason, Juan was going to miss me. The feeling was mutual. Perhaps I was the first person to take any real interest in him, or maybe he was lacking a father figure. Whatever the reason, there was no question that since we had started sponsoring him, Juan was growing attached to me and I to him.

All of the children were dear, yet there was definitely something special about Juan. I wanted to tell him that I cared deeply about him, but wasn't sure how to say it. In Spanish, you wouldn't generally say, "I love you," to anyone but your wife. Most would say, "te quiero," which means, "I want you." So I told Juan that I wanted him--I didn't know what else to say. At the time, I didn't realize that I could not have said anything more appropriate. Juan yearned to be wanted.

"Juan," I said, trying to get him to lift his head. I wanted to see his eyes, so that I could know if he understood me.

"If I have a son...." I began, trying to say it right with my limited Spanish. "If I have a son, I want him to be just like you." Then I added, "I would not change anything. Do you understand?"

Juan nodded, but continued to cry.

"You are very special..." I said, as a teacher called the children to class.

I had not planned to say those things--they had just come out. But I began to wonder whether I was setting us both up for heartbreak. After all, how could I possibly help a child from 2000 miles away?

I dreaded the thought of leaving Juan alone at Casa de Elizabeth again--but there was nothing else I could do. My week was up and it was time for me to go back home. Leaving was even harder the second time around, and neither Juan nor I could escape without many tears.

Although I couldn't promise him I would be back, I couldn't wait to return to that very special place.

CHAPTER TWENTY-THREE

* * *

A Step of Faith

* * *

And Peter answered him and said, Lord, if it be thou,
bid me come unto thee on the water.
And he said, Come...

Matthew 14:28-29

It was my first day back at work after returning from Imuris, and I was struggling to keep my mind on my work. Time and again, I found my thoughts wandering to Mexico.

Sitting at my desk, I picked up my daily Bible verse calendar and started tearing off a week's worth of pages. I was reading them one by one, when I came to Sunday, February 24, 2002. The verse on the calendar read:

"I know thy works: behold, I have set before thee an open door, and no man can shut it: for thou hast a little strength, and hast kept my word, and hast not denied my name." (Revelation 3:8 KJV)

Although I didn't know for sure what that meant, I saved the page and still have it with me today. It gave me the peace to know that I didn't need to have it all figured out. From then on, I knew that we didn't have to worry, because whatever was to be would be--and no one was going to stop it.

I was excited about the work in Mexico. Even though I didn't yet know what God's will was, I really felt it had something to do with this orphanage. However, my heart was also heavy because I cared deeply for Juan, and ached to help him in some way. The more I thought about it, the more I realized that if we were supposed to go to Mexico, many pieces would first need to fall into place.

Joy and I talked often about being involved in Mexico, and to this point, Joy had been really supportive, a good listener, and open to how the Lord would lead. I think that she too sensed something was happening.

Eventually, we both agreed that it was time for us to make the trip together and see what God had in store. Our minds still couldn't comprehend going to Mexico, but we knew that we had to search it out. It was at this point that we began to counsel with our close family.

The purpose of the trip would be to find out more about the need for a Bible teacher/counselor at Casa de Elizabeth. A missionary, who had been involved at the orphanage for several years, was leaving and there was a possibility that we could take his place. It looked like a door was opening for us to help.

Although we never liked to leave our girls, we did not feel at ease with the idea of taking them with us. Our plan was to stay at the orphanage, where the accommodations were not all that comfortable. So, in the end, we decided that just Joy and I would go.

From the outset, there appeared to be many obstacles that could make it difficult for us to ever serve in Mexico. One thing, that very few people knew, was that Joy and I had been approved for adoption and were waiting for a boy from South Korea. We had been working through the process for about a year and were expecting news about a child referral at any time.

When Joy and I were engaged to be married, we both thought that it would be nice to have a big family. Joy, especially, loved small children, which was one of the things that attracted me to her. After we married, we were disappointed when she didn't get pregnant the first month. We sure hadn't taken any precautions! Unlike some couples that prefer to wait to have children, Joy and I were ready to have them right away.

We were thrilled when Chloe arrived about a week after our first anniversary. But then there was a long, five-year wait for Salome. At times we were tempted to seek help, but Joy always felt that we had placed our desire to have children in God's hands, and if He wanted us to have more, we would. Joy also had the desire to adopt a child if we didn't have our own.

Then Salome came along. After Salome, we again counted off the years. Another five years passed, and we began to consider adoption--finally deciding to adopt a boy from South Korea.

The whole adoption process had been a little difficult for me, and I have to admit that I was not as enthusiastic as my wife. Even so, I was excited about having a son, which I think is something every man would like to have--whether he admits it or not.

In the beginning, it was hard for me to imagine adopting a child that I had never met, but by this point, I was pretty much over that. But there was one thing that did still bother me. We had changed agencies because the one we were with was way behind and having trouble making placements. The new agency promised that they could get a baby sooner, so we made the change. At that time we didn't realize that, because we had switched agencies, there was a stipulation that we would have to take a baby that may have some sort of imperfection

Later, when we did find out about this provision, I was somewhat bothered by the thought of them giving us an imperfect child. I had no idea what that would mean, or how the selection process would work, but as the months passed, I began to wonder if they were actually waiting for an "imperfect" one to come along so that they could give it to us. Something about the process and the change of agencies, which didn't save us any time after all, troubled me. I was never completely at peace about it.

Finally, one night I commented to Joy that I thought it would be easier for me to adopt a child I knew, rather than one I didn't. The child would be a "known quantity," so to speak, and I would know that I could love him.

Joy seemed to understand, so I mentioned Juan and how I would be willing to adopt a boy like him. It remained a mystery to me why an intelligent, talented boy like him would not be wanted. Of course, the suggestion was purely hypothetical, since I had no idea if it would even be possible to adopt Juan.

Naturally, Joy was not overly keen on the idea of adopting a 13-year-old boy. Although I understood her reluctance, I still pondered the thought, and asked that she keep an open mind until she had a chance to meet Juan herself. With a visit planned to Imuris for the two of us, Joy was soon to get that chance.

* * *

When we arrived at Casa de Elizabeth, the plan was that we would stay in Rick's quarters, as I had done before. This loving, self-less man insisted that we stay in his quarters, while he slept on the floor of the library. He had even tidied the place up, and the look on his face showed how proud he was of the improvement his cleaning had made. Even so, I could tell by the look on Joy's face that she was wondering what it must have looked like before.

Garbage bags were stacked almost to the roof, and junk was lying everywhere. Rick had swept what could be seen of the floor, and his Vietnam stuff, including ammunition boxes and his survival knives, were still on display. Thankfully, he had no M16's, as owning a gun is illegal in Mexico. Only the Mafioso drug traffickers and military had them.

Standing in the middle of Rick's cluttered room, in such a hot, dusty place, I couldn't help thinking that Joy was going beyond the call. She seemed to handle it all with such grace.

Later that night, just before we went to sleep, we talked about her first impressions, including her thoughts about Juan. Then I asked whether she would consider adopting him.

Earlier that day, Juan had welcomed us both with a big hug and smile. Then, accompanying himself on his guitar, he sang some beautiful Christian songs, which he later admitted he did because he knew it melted the hearts of American visitors. Although I knew that Juan had made a good first impression on my wife, I was still surprised when she responded that she would be willing to take him. She was willing to surrender her will to God's if He led us down that path.

With that decision made, we closed our eyes and fell asleep....

"Ah! Ah! Ah! Ah!"

Joy's shriek startled me awake, and I recognized the scream immediately. It was the same one she had used when she saw a mouse in the first house we rented in the country. I remember running into the kitchen, only to find her standing on the countertop. It was also the way she screamed at night when she had a bad dream. Whenever that happened, Joy would literally spring up in bed and jump on top of me.

Thankfully, in Rick's room, we were sleeping in separate cots, so Joy couldn't jump on top of me. But she was still jumping, while screaming, *"Get it! Get it! Kill it!"*

"What?" I finally managed to engage my vocal cords.

"It's a *huge* spider! Right there!" she said, pointing into the darkness.

"What are you talking about?" I asked; all traces of sleep completely gone. "It's pitch-black in here. How could you possibly see anything?"

"It's *there!*" she insisted. "I saw it!"

"How?" I questioned, turning on the flashlight. There was nothing lurking in the shadows.

"Ohhhh," Joy moaned and turned over in her bed. "It was sooo real."

"I'm sorry." There was nothing else I could say.

"I don't like this place."

"I know," I said. "Joy, you're being a *really* good sport."

And she was.

Throughout the months that followed, we both pondered what we felt was the calling of God to serve in Mexico. We knew that there was a need at Casa de Elizabeth for a couple, like us, to go and teach. For almost two years we had been praying for God's direction regarding His call for our lives, and at last it seemed clear where He was leading. Even so, there were some major obstacles to be overcome before we could answer that call.

Of all the obstacles, the biggest by far was the thought of the incredible change that would be involved in moving to Mexico, leaving our families, church, and friends behind. What would we do with our house and all our possessions? What about the planned, imminent adoption from South Korea? We had been waiting for over six months and a placement could happen at any time. How could we go to Mexico with a young child? What about our girls and their

health and safety? What about my work at FBi? What about financial support? Would the church support us? Would they send us?

The questions and problems seemed overwhelming ... but even
more so was the feeling that this was God's plan for our lives.

CHAPTER TWENTY-FOUR

* * *

Meeting Sara

* * *

Great Spirit, help me never to judge another
until I have walked in his moccasins.

–Sioux Indiana prayer

"Hot Tacos!" "Steaming hot tamales!" The shouts of street-side vendors filled the air as they carried their small coolers of Mexican-style fast-food in search of customers. In the midst of the sights and sounds of nighttime Imuris, Juan and I stood waiting for our bus to arrive.

It was April, 2002, and we had returned to the orphanage with our whole family for another one week visit. During this stay, I had arranged to go with Juan for a visit to his mother in Navojoa, which was something that I had been looking forward to for some time.

As we waited, another bus screeched to a halt a few feet from where we stood. The bus station in Imuris is a stark, cement building at the intersection of International Highway 15 and another state highway. A mixture of noises and smells lingered in the air, with Mexican music blaring from a set of overpowered speakers. The aroma of fried food wafted from a small stand on one side of the terminal. Even though most of the town had turned in for the night, the scene around the station was still very busy.

Every few minutes, buses pulled off the highway, coming to a grinding halt in a cloud of dust in front of the station. Sometimes more than one bus would arrive, and the drivers would have to park wherever they could find room. Before the dust cleared from their arrival, vendors would come running, jockeying for the best position to sell their food. There was a chaotic type of order.

I was excited to be making the trip with Juan, and anxious to learn more about his past--particularly why he was in the orphanage. Juan would never tell me much, and I didn't want to press him. So I figured that one way I could learn more was to meet his family and see his home for myself. Our plan was to take the bus at night, spend one day in Navojoa, and then return to Imuris that evening.

Weary travelers crowded the terminal, spilling out the door and down the walkway as Juan and I waited in line to ask about tickets. Finally it was our turn, and although I couldn't understand much of the conversation that developed, I could tell that it wasn't good news by the way the attendant was shaking his head.

It turned out that we had chosen a busy time to travel, and the attendant could not sell us a ticket until he knew whether there was room for us on any of the arriving buses.

We waited and waited, as bus after bus pulled into the station in a plume of dust, then left in a cloud of black exhaust. Each time we would think that it must be the one, only to be told, once again, that the bus was full.

After a couple of hours, I began to worry that we would never find a bus with room for two more passengers. All the time, I was relying on Juan to keep track of what was going on, because I wasn't able to understand the fast-talking attendant.

At long last, an old bus pulled in and, as had happened with the earlier arrivals, was quickly swamped by vendors. On seeing the absolutely terrible state of the 60's-style bus, my first reaction was that it had broken down. The engine door was propped open with a piece of wood, and I could see the steaming, oil-covered motor inside.

Seeing the bus, Juan jumped up from where we were sitting. As he did, all I could think was, "Surely not *that* one!" From the look of it, I didn't think the vehicle would make it out of town, let alone the long, eight hour trip to Navojoa!

Juan asked me for money, which he then gave to a man. In turn, that man gave part of the money to another man. I watched it go from hand to hand, wondering if the payment would eventually turn into a ticket, or if I had just made some sort of donation. By that point, I wasn't even sure that I wanted a ticket on *that* bus at all. I would have gladly paid a little more for a seat on a newer, more-reliable looking one, rather than taking the risk of a midnight breakdown in the middle of the desert.

In the end, we never did get an actual ticket, but they did motion us on board. Go figure. So we grabbed our bags and then fought through the shoulder-to-shoulder crowd to the door.

Reaching the bus, we climbed the steps and entered the dark aisle, only to discover that the bus was completely full--all except for one seat.

My heart sank. It was almost midnight, and we were both so tired. There was no way that we could wait for another bus. We both stood there for a moment, wondering who should get the seat. Then a woman with a baby climbed on board, and that solved that problem!

Juan and I went to the rear of the bus and sat down in the narrow aisle. I leaned back against the motor cover, which was hard, hot, and noisy. The smell of all the various body odors had been bad enough as we had walked down the aisle, but that was nothing compared to the pungent odor which radiated from the bathroom door alongside my position next to the motor.

It was then that I half thought about jumping up and getting off. But before I had time to turn the thought into action, there was a grinding noise and the bus lunged forward. Although I was glad to be on our way, I couldn't help wondering how we would survive the eight hour journey.

Deciding to make the best of a bad situation, I tried to make myself as comfortable as was possible for a person sitting on a ridge in a hard, gritty floor. I was not successful. Juan, on the other hand, obviously didn't share my discomfort. He immediately stretched out on the floor, laid his head by my leg, and in less than a minute, was fast asleep.

I was amazed at Juan's ability to sleep through all the transmission noise and engine vibrations. Then I realized that a childhood spent sleeping in a noisy one room house, on dirt floors and wooden beds would make it easier to sleep almost anywhere. In this case, I wasn't quite so fortunate. I had grown up with coveted comforts, but now I was a bit envious for how this boy was so adaptable.

Half an hour later, the bus made its first stop, and two people got off. Without waiting for an invitation, we quickly jumped from the floor and raced to the empty seats. Although sleep still eluded me, at least I was finally able to rest.

The sun was just coming over the horizon when we arrived in Navojoa, and already it was hot. Juan's family home was in a poor area far from the center of town, so I hired a taxi and we headed on our way.

As we traveled toward the edge of town, the condition of the houses became worse and worse. As I looked at the deteriorating landscape, I found it almost impossible to believe that people were actually living in cardboard shacks in the middle of the desert.

Juan said that it wasn't really a problem until it rained. Then, because the ground was so flat, people often ended up with as much as 2 feet of water in their homes. Even worse, the wind would some-times come and flatten homes to the ground. Not surprisingly, Juan explained that the people were terrified of storms because their homes provided no real shelter.

By the time we reached Juan's neighborhood, the homes looked like they had been built the day before using whatever scraps could be found lying around.

Juan's house was no exception. It was about 15 feet square, made of black tarpaper, and had a flat, tin roof. Situated on a small, dirt lot on a dirt street, the home was basically in the middle of the desert. There were no trees, no bushes, and no running water. As I absorbed the sight of my young friend's home, my first thought was, "You've got to be kidding!" It was impossible for me to believe that anyone could live in such conditions for a week, let alone years.

The interior was no better. Entering the small shack, I glanced around at the meager furnishings. Three wooden beds took up most of the real estate, their legs set on rocks on the hard-packed dirt floor. A clothes cabinet stood in one corner of the room, with a small TV above it. In the other corner, a variety of cooking utensils hung on nails over a table.

The dirt yard was neat, and I could tell that it had been swept, perhaps in preparation for our visit. The outhouse was no more than a few scraps around a wooden box, which was perched over a hole in the ground. Even from a distance, the stench was offensive, and I prayed that I wouldn't have the necessity to use it during our stay.

On the other side of the lot, there was a clothes-washing station and another enclosure which served as the shower.

As soon as we arrived, Sara kissed her son, hugging him close to her heart. It was clearly obvious that she genuinely loved her boy. After welcoming Juan home, she smiled briefly in my direction, revealing a row of deformed teeth. Then, with gracious hospitality, Sara offered me the most pathetic excuse for a chair I had ever seen. It was an old, rusty, tube-frame with a plank of wood wired on for a seat, and no seat back.

Although I was shocked by the severe poverty of my surroundings, I was also impressed by Juan's mother. Sara had graciously greeted me with kindness and respect, and I could tell that she was an intelligent and thoughtful woman. I could also tell that she was as anxious as I was to talk, so while Juan ran off down the street, Sara and I sat down to chat.

Bit by bit, over the next hour or so, I learned a little more about Juan's life. I had always been interested to know more about my young friend, because I cared about him. However, I had also always been sensitive to the fact that this was a private matter which may, possibly, be too painful for him to talk about.

As we talked, Sara would only say that her son's past was very sad, and that she had lost him. With a loving mother's pride, she told me that Juan was very special. Then she sadly explained how, as a last resort to save him, she had made the hard decision to send him away.

Sara then showed me the letter that Juan had written to her, telling her that he had an American friend. With transparent honesty, she told me that she had been so excited to read this, because that had been the heartfelt hope she had carried for her son. In fact, Sara admitted that she had sent Juan to an orphanage in the north so that he would be close to the US border, in the hope that he may meet an American who would want to help him.

I could hardly believe my ears. There I was, 2000 miles from home, sitting with a Mexican woman of about my own age, who had been praying for me--an unknown American--to come and rescue her son. It was awe inspiring ... and humbling.

All the while we were talking, Juan was running around outside, playing soccer and having a ball; acting like the most normal, adorable child in the world. He seemed so very happy to be home, and as I watched him playing, I wondered again if, perhaps, this wasn't the best place for him to be. Even after talking to Sara, I still didn't understand why Juan shouldn't be with his mother, and this question conflicted with the growing feeling that we were meant to help him--possibly even adopt him. As this mental battle raged, I finally turned to Sara and asked her what it was that she wanted us to do.

During our conversation, Sara and I had made frequent use of a pad and pencil in order to help with our communication. Reaching for it again, Sara wrote that her dream was for her son to be able to go to school in the United States.

As she shared her hope, I nodded and promised to look into whether it would be possible.

It wasn't until after my visit with Sara, that it hit me that if Juan did come to live with us in the US, it would mean that we wouldn't be able to return to Mexico for a few years. This left me wondering as to the right course of action for our family. Although I was sure that God wanted us to make the move, I wasn't at all sure when that move was meant to be. It was then that I started to consider the possibility that He may actually want us to wait for a while.

After we returned home, I tried every conceivable way to get a visa for Juan--without success. I called congressmen and senators, and even went as far as trying to get our local school registered to accept foreign exchange students from Mexico. In spite of my efforts, every avenue resulted in a dead-end. Although I had done everything I could, it just wasn't possible to bring Juan to the United States. The door wasn't just closed ... it was slammed shut!

Once all options had been exhausted, I wrote a letter to Sara explaining what had happened. Then I told her that the only way Juan could possibly come to the US was if we legally adopted him as our son.

I hadn't necessarily wanted to suggest adoption, but by that point could see that it really was the only way to fulfill Sara's dream of a US education for her boy.

Even so, I felt that my question had been answered. As Juan was not able to come to us, it was obviously all the more reason for us to go to him in Mexico--and sooner rather than later.

CHAPTER TWENTY-FIVE

* * *

Hearing the Call

* * *

Happiness comes of the capacity to feel deeply,
to enjoy simply, to think freely, to risk life,
to be needed.

–Storm Jameson

In June of 2002, Joy and I took, what was for us, the big step of talking to the Mission Committee of our church. We honestly admitted that we didn't really feel prepared to be missionaries, but wanted to share with them what we felt the Lord had placed on our hearts. We also wanted to seek their advice as to how we should proceed.

With kindness, understanding and support, the Committee members suggested that we go to Imuris for one month as a family, and then report back to them on our return home.

Although we had, only two months earlier, spent one week there as a family, Joy and I agreed that it would be a good idea to see how we all coped with being there for a longer period of time. So, with that goal in mind, we planned to make a return trip to Imuris for the whole month of September. This decision was another major leap toward a long term move to Mexico.

* * *

During the summer before our trip, I found that I had a lot of time to think when I was out mowing our grass. One of the things that often came to mind was the ongoing situation with the sale of AdaptaSoft. Financially, things were not going all that well, which meant that the employees who were buying the company were not able to pay me what they had said they would.

Under the terms of our agreement, I was to receive a minimum amount each year, for a number of years, in lieu of payment up front. My plan in selling the company this way was to have this minimum amount to live off while we were working in the mission field. With the uncertainty of not clearly knowing what we would be doing, I was counting on this payment for our regular income. Yet, even after closing our first deal, nagging concerns started to trouble me. In the end, these unsettling concerns were a contributing factor to my eventual decision to work at FBi.

Unfortunately, before long, those concerns proved to be valid. As soon as AdaptaSoft began having cash flow problems, the payments stopped. Then, I had to renegotiate the contract, and this time there were no minimum payments. Although we agreed on a new contract that we designed to help the new owners, I continued to have doubts that we would ever receive much of anything as a result of the sale of the business.

Although I was really thankful to be out of the payroll business, I have to admit that the situation did bother me to some extent. I had always thought my primary concern was for the welfare of my previous employees, AdaptaSoft's customers, and the company as a whole. I was more concerned about those things than I was about my own welfare--at least, that's what I kept telling myself. But I was also worried about our own financial interests. God was about to show me that I wasn't being completely honest with myself.

Then one day as I was thinking and praying about these things while mowing our large lawn, God showed me that I needed to surrender our finances to Him. He showed me that I had to stop worrying about whether or not AdaptaSoft would ever pay me anything. I had to let it go and just trust in God. If we were going to go to the mission field, I had to have enough faith that He would provide everything we would need.

More than that, He made it clear that I needed to surrender all the money we had made in the past, together with all that we would earn in the future. It was all His--and nothing really mattered if we truly trusted Him to provide.

By God's grace, I was able to surrender our finances to the Lord--and what a great relief it was to do that. I no longer had to worry about AdaptaSoft, because I had faith to believe that God would take care of everything. Now I really could be concerned for the welfare of my former employees. I began to pray more sincerely for them.

On that day, I was able to surrender our house, together with its big green yard, our car, and all our possessions. This was another great step in the direction of our going to Mexico. To make that final move, we would need to be able to leave everything behind--and at that moment, in my mind, I had done exactly that. Another piece of the puzzle had fallen into place.

* * *

As the months passed and the decision of whether to go to Mexico or not became unavoidable, there was a fair amount of controversy about it. However, the majority of people we talked to were very supportive.

With the ongoing distraction of Mexico always with me, one would think that my employer would have been quite happy to see me go. But in spite of my distraction, they were very understanding and encouraging. This was probably largely due to the fact that I had been upfront with them from the start about my belief that God was calling us to some form of mission work. Another lesser reason may have been because it had been my friendship with an FBi coworker that had led to my initial involvement in the World Relief effort.

During my last year with the company, I spent many weeks in Mexico, and FBi made that possible by allowing me to take vacation days, personal days, and leave without pay.

There was also a great deal of support from the church. When we told our retired elder--a brother who had played an instrumental part in our lives when Joy and I were younger--he was very encouraging. One night, after church, I began explaining to him how we felt God was calling us to Mexico. Before I had a chance to finish, he interrupted me with a huge, loving smile, put an encouraging hand on my shoulder, and simply said, "Go!"

"When you get older like me, you wish you had taken more risks and done more," he explained. "If I could, I would go with you--but

I can't now. You're young enough that you can. As long as you stay pliable and teachable--which I'm sure you will--you can be a great blessing in Mexico, as well as for our church here."

This positive encouragement was echoed by our current elder and the other ministers.

During this time, as we contemplated the call to go, Joy and I were amazed at how God was clearly leading us to Mexico through our personal devotions. At almost every church service there would be something in the sermon, or a prayer, or one of the songs we sang, that touched our hearts and pointed us south of the border.

Songs like "Ready to go, ready to stay, ready to do His will," and "Anywhere with Jesus," seemed to speak directly to us. Chapters in the Bible, such as Matthew 25, 28 and Acts 1 took on all new meaning. It seemed so obvious, that we commented that it was as if God was calling the whole Francesville church!

The hardest thing, though, was thinking about leaving our families, friends, and home church. I was especially torn at the thought of leaving Mom, as she had been very lonely since Dad passed away. I knew that our two girls, in particular, were a blessing that brightened her day whenever we visited--which was quite often. Mom was not happy about the thought of being separated from us, yet she still supported our decision to follow God's leading, even though it was a huge sacrifice for her.

Joy's family was also supportive, having a history of being mission-minded. However, even for them it was a big sacrifice, because the family is so close-knit, and family gatherings have always been such a blessing.

But every day that passed, we were being drawn closer and closer southward in answer to God's call.

CHAPTER TWENTY-SIX

* * *

A New Son?

* * *

The greatest use of life is to spend it for
something that will outlast it.

–William James

Early in July, 2002, I made another week-long trip to Imuris, and during that time, Juan and I took a quick trip by bus to Navojoa to talk with his mother. Although I had written to Sara, I wanted to explain to her, face to face, that I had tried every way imaginable to get a visa for Juan, but it just hadn't been possible. I had found that even the process of making enquiries was often frustrating, apparently due to the changes in attitude and rules following the 9-11 disaster.

In the process of my enquiries, I had also looked into the possibility of adopting Juan as a way to get him across the border. Again, I found that this was almost impossible because of corruption on the Mexican side, and prejudice on the American side. With so much working against it, instigating an adoption was simply not worth even trying. Apparently, there were only a handful of successful adoptions between the two countries each year, and there wasn't a single US agency that would handle a Mexican adoption.

So, with every other option blocked, my plan was to explain to Sara that we felt God was calling us to move to Mexico to help in the orphanage in Imuris, and that it was our hope to be able to help Juan from there. With his mother's permission, I thought that we could have legal custody of him, and that he would then live with us as part of our family.

That was my plan, but when we arrived in Navojoa, before I had a chance to share with Sara, she took Juan aside for a long talk. When they came back, they were both excited to tell me something.

"Go ahead," Sara encouraged her son.

"No, you," Juan replied hesitantly.

"No, you should tell him," Sara insisted with a grand smile.

Juan was smiling too, but acting really shy about telling me whatever it was they were so excited about. I began to wonder what could possibly be so important or difficult to tell.

"No, I can't," the boy insisted.

"Yes you can," his mother reassured, before repeating, "go ahead."

By this time, I found myself wanting to say, *"Just tell me!"*

"Oh ... OK," Juan finally relented after a long pause.

He motioned for me to bend down so he could say something in my ear. Then he grabbed my shoulder and whispered, "You are going to be my dad."

"What?" I asked, not sure that I'd heard correctly.

"You are going to adopt me," Juan said. Then he peered into my face as if watching for my reaction. Sara was beaming, hands clasped in front of her.

"You want us to adopt Juan?!" I repeated in disbelief.

All heads nodded, eyes wide with excitement.

Suddenly I realized what had happened. Knowing that legal adoption was the only way for her son to get to the United States, to get a good education and have a good life, Sara had decided to give Juan to us. I was shocked, and didn't know what to say.

It wasn't that she didn't love Juan; in fact, it was quite the opposite. Sara had decided to do this because she loved him so much and cared more for his wellbeing than her own happiness. She had already given her son away once before, when she had sent him far away to Imuris, but now she was prepared to do it again. This brave woman was willing to send Juan somewhere so far away that she would never even be able to travel to see him.

I was totally overwhelmed and confused! On one hand, I loved this boy who was looking at me as though I was the father he had always wanted. In my eyes, he too was so special, and the thought of being his father thrilled my heart.

On the other hand, I was terrified--for many reasons. Firstly, by this time, we were almost sure that we would be moving to Mexico, so adopting Juan would not get him to the US. Secondly, I had looked into adoption in Mexico and knew that it was practically impossible for Americans to do. Thirdly, we were in the process of waiting for a South Korean baby, which was, in fact, overdue and could arrive at any moment!

I glanced at Sara and then back at Juan. I saw the conviction on the faces of mother and son. I knew that they had already made their decision. Saying "no" was just not possible. I couldn't begin to imagine how Juan must have felt at that moment. After just 10 minutes with his mother, they had made a decision that could change his life forever.

This boy had already been rejected by two fathers, and I was not going to do that to him again. I could not ... I would not. Not only because I didn't want to, but because it was something that simply must not be done.

I still had not said anything and now Juan's big, brown eyes were searching my face for a response. "You do want me, don't you?" they seemed to ask.

After what must have seemed like an eternity for Juan, I smiled and took him in my arms. It was the answer he was looking for. He wrapped his arms around me too. I motioned for Sara to join in, and we all hugged each other and enjoyed that special moment together.

I didn't have a clue what I was going to do, but had a feeling that Juan was going to be a part of our family. Given the circumstances, what else could I have done?

Not surprisingly, I felt like I needed to talk to Joy right away, so asked where we could find a public phone. Sara said there was one nearby, but we ended up walking for what seemed like a mile in the intensely hot, midday sun.

I was exhausted by the time I finally made it to the metal pay phone, but the handset was too hot to handle with my bare hands. Even so, I managed to call Joy and tell her just a few words. Then I hung up the receiver, and we started the long walk back. Although I was in pretty good physical shape, I still had to stop and rest in the shade as the sheer heat was overwhelming.

When we finally made it back to the house, I collapsed on one of the beds and fell fast asleep.

Before long, it was time for us to head back to Imuris. As we walked through Sara's poor neighborhood on our way back to the bus stop, we could see a dark storm approaching over the desert, with towering clouds, lightning and rain. It was heading our way, and its arrival appeared to be imminent. Ahead of it, a cooler breeze had picked up, which was unusual for the normally dry, oven-like desert climate.

I was amazed to see that every other shack owner was up on his roof, pounding nails. It literally sounded like the whole neighborhood was under construction. As I watched their activity, I wondered if this was normal storm preparation, but thought that if there were roof repairs to be done, they probably shouldn't have all waited until the last minute.

Reaching the bus stop, I stood for a moment and admired the beautiful colors of the rapidly darkening sky, which made a startling backdrop for the sheer poverty of the neighborhood. The contrast was extreme, as were the dramatic events that had just transpired in our lives. It was all too much for me to comprehend.

As the storm rumbled closer, Sara said goodbye to her son, and then, as the first drops of rain began raising the dust on the ground, and our bus appeared in the distance, she turned and raced for home.

Moments later, Juan and I were on the bus and heading back to the center of town.

* * *

The nine hour trip back to Imuris gave me plenty of time to think--time that I desperately needed. As the storm continued to rage, and the rain smacked against the cold glass of the bus window, my heart was torn. Over and over again, I silently asked, *"What have I done?!"* I had no idea how I was going to explain this sudden change of plans to Joy.

As my thoughts tumbled over themselves, I thought about the storm that was brewing outside. Even though it would bring blessed rain and relief from the heat, it was also very intimidating and scary. Staring out at the black sky, I realized that a similar storm was brewing within me. On one hand, I was excited about the idea of Juan being our son. On the other hand, the thought of adopting a 13-year-old was preposterous. There was no way I could expect Joy to adopt a teenage boy instead of a baby!

But how could we deny this boy and his mother?

Sara had insisted that we visit the office of the Mexican Adoption Authority--the DIF--in order to get things started straight away. We did this, and to my surprise, everyone we spoke to at the DIF said that the process was actually quite straightforward and legal.

This did not fit with the information I had already received, and so I had tried to tell them how difficult it really was. In response, they handed me a list of requirements, and assured me that it was indeed possible for an American to adopt Juan. In fact, they indicated that there shouldn't be any problem at all, as all parties were in favor of the adoption. That being the case, they made the amazing prediction that the process should only take a few months once I had submitted the appropriate paperwork.

As the bus to Imuris continued to bounce through the storm, I continued to struggle with my thoughts. Even if it was possible for us to adopt Juan--which I still doubted--the reality was that we were expecting a baby, and I knew that was what Joy really wanted. She liked Juan, but a 13-year-old is hardly the same as an infant.

Although Joy had been open to the idea of adopting Juan when we had first discussed the possibility, things now seemed to have become a lot more complicated. For one thing, there was the supposedly imminent Korean adoption to take into consideration, not to mention the major issue of us probably going out on the mission field. With our lives so up in the air about moving to Mexico, any adoption plans at all were questionable.

"Bap?"

My stream of thoughts were interrupted by the sound of Juan saying my name. Then he smiled and affectionately said, "Papá?"

"What?" I asked, mentally shaking my mind away from the problem of how I was going to tell Joy.

Juan's wide eyes told me that he was about to say something important. "This storm..." he began, thoughtfully. "It reminds me of one time when I was at the orphanage. There was a big storm and I was all alone, and I cried out to God for help."

I nodded, encouraging him to go on. He shared more details, and we laughed and giggled about how he had gone running from the lightning, and hidden from God in his bed. But then Juan got serious.

"Well, I just wanted you to know that, uh ... that *you came right after that.*"

He didn't say it, but I knew what he was thinking--I was the answer to his prayer. We were both realizing that this whole thing--our coming to the orphanage, meeting, the adoption, everything--was no accident.

We sat there in silence, listening to the storm and hiss of rain outside, as we pondered and wondered. Then Juan laid his head on my shoulder and went quickly to sleep.

Although I was bone weary, I still couldn't sleep. I had taken a nap that afternoon at Juan's house, which is about the only thing you can do in the heat of the day, but that was all the sleep I had been able to get in two days.

As Juan slept, my thoughts went back to my childhood--to the Mexican family that lived in a trailer near our home. This family had been special to me because they had a daughter named Michelle, who was in my third grade class. With her dark hair and skin, I thought Michelle was the most beautiful girl I had ever seen. So I spent time playing with her and her younger brothers for the short time that they lived near us.

We didn't have very many Mexicans living in our town, and I was intrigued by their language, and the differences I saw. I rarely saw Michelle's father--in fact, we never met. Her mother always stayed inside, probably because she didn't speak English. Sadly, there was no one to befriend her, because no one in town spoke Spanish.

Michelle's mother was an artist, and drew beautiful pictures. I still remember Michelle showing some of them to me.

During the time that Michelle and her family lived near our home, we had a lot of fun playing together. Even though we were

176

just little kids, I felt a special attraction to my classmate and her brothers.

Then one day, the family just packed up and left. Michelle told me that they were leaving, and then I watched them drive away. I ran to the edge of the highway, following them as far as I could. When I could go no further, I just stood there with tears in my eyes, watching as their truck grew smaller and smaller. The whole time I hoped that they would turn around--but they never did.

I never saw Michelle again, but I always dreamed of meeting her again some day. After that, I always paid special attention to Hispanic people, hoping that maybe, just maybe, it would be Michelle or her family.

Suddenly, the brakes of the bus groaned as we came to a stop. A military officer boarded the vehicle, and began asking questions and searching bags. I had been warned about these officials. It was well know that even though they were looking for drug smugglers, they would sometimes steal while they were looking through bags. For a moment, I wondered what I would do if this particular officer tried to steal from me, but then I decided that I probably wouldn't argue with a man carrying an automatic weapon. Instead, I pretended to be asleep, and started to pray that he wouldn't ask me anything, or check my bags.

It worked. He passed me by, and was soon off the bus, leaving us free to continue our journey north.

Once again, my thoughts returned to Juan and the adoption issue. I remembered a particular day in college when I had been alone in our apartment on Harrison Street. Although I had studies to do, I didn't feel like doing them. I had just gotten back from class, and was lying on the couch, thinking, praying, and feeling lonely.

At that time, I had been 20 years old, and was thinking about my future and the things that I would like to do after I graduated. A whole lot of unknowns ran through my head--Would I get married? If I did, what would my wife be like? Would we have children?

Then it hit me! All of a sudden I remembered that I had even thought about adopting a boy from Mexico.

As the memory of that day flooded back, I thought, *"How strange that I would think that way back then. I wonder why?"*

Maybe the original idea had come because of the love I had felt for Michelle and her family. Then again, maybe it had been God planting the first seed of a thought in my heart. If that was the case, then I wondered why I would have had this premonition while I was still in college--and not even married.

Then I realized that, as I was 20 years older than Juan, it was quite possible that he had been born at the same time that I had been thinking about my future. Could it be that, 13 years earlier, God had put this thought in my mind as he breathed life into this child? A child whose future He knew would be troubled? I trembled at the thought.

Now He was bringing Juan into our family, and I was in awe. I felt so small--so helpless and powerless to affect divinely planned events. Even with this revelation, I still didn't know what I was going to tell Joy. But now I sensed that it was God's will that we adopt this boy. Regardless of the fact that this was actually what I wanted, in light of this revelation of divine direction, I couldn't see how it could possibly be avoided.

The words from Revelation coursed through my mind, *"Behold, I have set before thee an open door, and no man can shut it."* [1] Somehow I knew that Joy was going to agree to adopt Juan. With that understanding, I felt a strange peace come over me, and I finally drifted off to sleep.

[1] Revelation 3:8 King James Version

CHAPTER TWENTY-SEVEN

* * *

A Change of Plans

* * *

We can do no great things – only small things
with great love.

–Mother Teresa

"What are you thinking about?" Joy asked, handing me a glass to dry.

We were washing dishes in the kitchen while the girls played on the computer in the school room.

"You can probably guess," I replied, knowing that Joy had to be able to read my thoughts. Here we were standing in a gorgeous kitchen, with tile and hardwood floors, raspberry stained woodwork, stainless steel appliances, and recessed lighting. The kitchen opened into the dining room and living room, which also had custom wood columns, marble accents, and a mirror above the fireplace that went all the way to the 18-foot ceiling. Our beautiful home was everything that anyone could ever want, and yet all I could think about was Mexico.

"You know, I can understand now why people get a divorce," I said, getting Joy's full attention. "I had never understood how it could happen, but now I do."

"What do you mean?" Joy stopped washing the plate in the sink, and looked quizzically in my direction.

"I mean, I love you, and I can't imagine anything ever changing that. There has never been anything to even make me think of not wanting to be with you."

Joy gave me a loving peck on the cheek, then asked, "So, I still don't understand why you brought up about divorce."

"It's just that I'm so thankful you feel the same as I do about Mexico. I feel so strongly about it, that if you didn't, I think it would tear us apart. Do you know what I mean?"

Joy considered this for a moment, then said, "But if it really is of God, then we should feel the same way--shouldn't we?"

"Yes ... but I know some Christian men who feel called, and their wives don't. That would be so hard."

It had been almost 24 hours since I arrived home from Imuris, and I was still looking for the right time to talk to Joy about adopting Juan. I was worried about what she would say, but knew that we had to talk about it soon.

"Joy, I was going to talk to you about this last night when I got home, but it was so late. I decided to wait until today to tell you, when we had more time."

"What is it?"

"Something incredible happened while I was visiting with Juan's mother," I began. "You know how we've talked about adopting Juan?"

Joy nodded cautiously, then said, "When you rang from Navojoa, you told me that she had asked us to adopt him."

"I know, but it was more than that. It's hard to explain ... it was the way it happened. They didn't even give me a chance to think about it, let alone call you to talk about it or anything! And even if they had, I really don't think I would have known how to say no."

"You didn't say we would--did you?" Joy's gaze worried me.

"Well, no, but what was I supposed to say? They didn't ask. They just assumed we would."

Joy was quiet.

"If you could have seen Juan's face after he said, 'You're going to be my father,' you would understand that there wasn't any way that I could have said no."

My wife nodded her understanding.

"But I feel bad about it. I don't think it's fair to you," I admitted. "You have waited so long for a baby--and Juan is not exactly a baby. I don't know what to say other than I feel like it is God's will that we put the Korean adoption on hold and adopt Juan first."

Sadness washed over Joy's face, and she lowered her head before giving a slight nod.

"But that's not all," I continued. "On the bus ride home, Juan shared how he had prayed for help--and then we arrived. It seems so incredible, so ridiculous to even think about adopting a thirteen-year-old, but that's what I feel we're supposed to do."

Looking up, Joy commented, "You never have been totally at peace about the Korean adoption, have you?"

"I never knew why," I admitted. "But maybe this is the reason."

Then I went on to explain about the premonition I had had when I was in college.

"It's so strange that I haven't remembered it until now--but now it's as clear as if it had happened yesterday."

I paused for a moment, then said, "But I really want to know what you think. I feel so bad about putting the baby on hold, and I don't want this to be something you hold against me, or for it to become something that comes between us."

"Bob, you don't need to worry about it," she reassured me. "Haven't we always put things like this in God's hands? Yes, I have waited a long time, but it's what God wants that really matters--not just what I want."

As I put my arms around her, Joy continued, "I just want us to always be in agreement on how to raise him."

I agreed without hesitation, and then Joy reasoned, "We need to talk to the girls, and see how they feel about it."

Any concerns we may have had that the girls might not have liked the idea, disappeared when we told them. They were both excited about having Juan as a big brother, because they both liked him. Even so, we could see that 10-year-old Chloe also felt very insecure about the idea of Juan taking her place as the oldest child in the family.

"Does that mean his name will come first in the church phone book?" she asked.

Much to her relief, we assured Chloe that we would always make sure that her name was first, since she came first.

* * *

After that, we felt as though we had to make a decision about Mexico, for several reasons. For one thing, I would need to give notice at my work, as I didn't feel right continuing to take time off without letting them know what our future plans were.

We also needed to talk to the agency that was handling the Korean adoption. If we were going to go to Mexico, then we would have no choice but to put this adoption request on hold. This was because one of the requirements of the adoption was that we could not leave the country for at least a year after receiving the child. We didn't know why it was taking so long for us to receive a placement, and we had no idea how much longer it was going to be. Having looked forward to this new arrival for so long already, it was an agonizing decision for us to make.

As our direction became clearer, we started to feel that it was too soon to make a long-term decision about moving permanently to Mexico. Instead, we decided to pray about going for two years, and then decide later whether to return home, or stay longer. Although I couldn't imagine returning after such a relatively short time, we decided to leave that possibility open--and those that we counseled with believed that this was a wise decision.

Another reason for an initial two-year stay was that it would give us enough time to process Juan's adoption, while still allowing the option to proceed with the Korean one later.

So, one day after supper, it was this plan that we put to prayer. We had been talking about how we both believed that God was leading us, but wanted a clear answer so that we could be at peace about our decision. With that in mind, Joy and I knelt down by the sofa in our living room and prayed a simple prayer that God would show us His will. Then I opened the Bible to Acts 7, and our eyes fell on verse 3:

> *"And said unto him, Get thee out of thy country, and from thy kindred, and come into the land which I shall shew thee."*

This was the first time that we had specifically asked for an answer. We weren't in the habit of doing that, but after six months of feeling led in that direction, we knew that it was time to ask. When we did, we had an immediate peace about going to Mexico for two years, and also about leaving the rest to the Lord.

With that peace and sense of confirmation, we called the adoption agency and asked them to put the Korean adoption on hold. Then we also started the process to change our home study, as well as preparing the paperwork to adopt Juan in Mexico.

Now we knew that we were going to Mexico--but we just didn't know when. Ahead of us there was still the one month, family trip in September, at the Mission Committee's suggestion. So we set our sights on that, and prepared to test the waters.

It was an interesting time in the lead up to our departure in September. Although we were now sure that we would eventually be going for at least two years, many of our friends and relatives began to express some doubts--and considering the history of brethren being sent on mission trips by our church, they had good reason. At that time, very few had been sent, so it was almost unheard of for the church to send a family like ours. Considering that we weren't the most qualified, we could understand their concerns--but we were willing, and we knew that we had been called.

"Do you really think they are going to give you permission to go?" was the question that we were most often asked. Each time, we replied that we believed they would.

Then they would say, "And what if they don't? Then what will you do?"

It was a question that we really hadn't given a great deal of thought. For one time in my life, I was actually trusting God, and believing in faith.

The same questions continued, time and time again, and it was clear that many thought we would never go to Mexico--that we were crazy to think there was a chance. In spite of their attitudes, throughout this time of waiting, we had peace. Joy and I both felt that not only would we be going, but we would be going long term. By saying it was for two years, we found that it was easier to explain to people, as well as making it easier for our loved ones, and ourselves, to handle.

But as far as we were concerned, God had made His will clear, and that being the case, I couldn't imagine the church not being on the same page.

CHAPTER TWENTY-EIGHT

* * *

One Month in September

* * *

Happiness is essentially a state of going somewhere,
wholeheartedly, one-directionally, without regret
or reservation.

–William H. Sheldon

September finally arrived and, with our minivan loaded to the ceiling, we headed for the border.

Thirty hours later, we finally arrived at Casa de Elizabeth in Imuris. The new volunteer house, where we would be living during our stay, was not yet finished. When we arrived, the house had no running water, no sinks, and no beds--in fact, there was very little furniture at all. We very quickly learned to live one day at a time, and find the best way to get by.

In the US, I wouldn't have thought twice about throwing away a 5-gallon bucket. But during our first month in Mexico, we treasured every one of the few buckets we had. Never before had I appreciated just how many important uses there are for a bucket. We used them for obvious things, like taking a bath and carrying water, as well as for other things, such as tool boxes, chairs, step-stools, trash bins, and food containers.

It didn't take long for us to realize that we had taken so many simple things for granted before coming to Mexico--things that we now had to do without. Our residence at the orphanage didn't have such comforts as air-conditioning, beds, mattresses, hot and cold running water, tables, chairs, or even window screens. Yet, we were still better off than our neighbors.

I found it almost impossible to believe that the orphanage didn't have a single hammer, screwdriver, or pair of pliers. Although I was handy around the house, I had never had a very good collection of tools. Even so, I had packed the little that I had into a small shoebox, and brought them with me to Mexico. As limited as my collection was, I think I had the best set in town. That being so, it wasn't long before people started knocking at our door to "borrow" my tools. Unfortunately, the tools I lent didn't come back. So very soon, I was in the same challenging, tool-less situation as everyone else!

It was then that I realized that to "lend" in Spanish must really mean to "give without ever expecting it back." There was a certain sense of guilt that you were expected to feel because you owned something that someone else needed. Because of this, you were obliged to give it away.

Having "given away" all my tools, I found it very frustrating trying to get any work done around the orphanage.

It was frustrating trying to work without tools. Once I even cut my hand, because I had "lent" my screwdriver to someone, and so was left with only a pair of pliers to try and remove a screw. My helper suggested that I try using my teeth, but I decided against that idea. Evidently, Mexican teeth are a lot stronger than mine. They can be used to do things like taking bottle tops off, while I cringe at the thought of even trying.

Inconveniences and missing tools aside, it was not surprising that I threw myself into this new effort in the same way that I had done with all my previous jobs. However, this time it was a little different. This time Joy and I were spending more time together, and were working together as a team. Our main priorities were to learn the language, start Bible classes, make our living quarters livable, and get to know Juan.

Learning Spanish was an intense, all day affair. No one at the orphanage spoke English, so we were in constant training. I went to bed with a headache almost every night, but by God's grace we did all learn the language very quickly.

That's not to say that we didn't make many mistakes--we did, and they were often embarrassing ones! I made many people laugh with my folly. I had the misfortune of saying "I have a man," when I meant to say "I'm hungry." I also said "I'm in heat," rather than "I'm hot," and "I'm pregnant," instead of "I'm embarrassed." If you are familiar with Spanish, you will be able to figure out how I made those errors, because the words are very similar.

We thoroughly enjoyed giving Bible classes to the various age groups, and ran about half a dozen classes each week. The younger ages were fairly easy, but the teenage classes required much more preparation. I would spend up to six hours preparing for a single lesson, which included learning new vocabulary, songs, games and other activities, all in Spanish.

With our goal to make our quarters livable, one of the first projects I tackled was putting up shelves in the kitchen for food, dishes and other things. Easier said than done.

With that project at the top of the list, I headed to town to look for brackets. It was then that I realized that not many Mexicans have shelving, in fact, no one seemed to even know the word for "shelf." This was, perhaps, not surprising when I considered that the average Mexican home does not have a lot of stuff to put on shelves in the first place.

In the US, any Home Depot store would probably stock hundreds of different shelf brackets. They come in plastic, wood, and metal of every size, design, and color you could imagine. In Mexico, I found one metal type--black in color, and available in two sizes.

One simply cannot imagine the difference in selection of products that there is between the two countries. In the US, we have super-stores that are filled from floor to ceiling with variety and quality. In Mexico, it is hard to find quality or any great range of selection--although, it is improving. Back home, I was accustomed to going to town with a list of ten items, and coming home with most, if not all, of them. In Mexico, I think I'm doing well if I'm able to find three out of the ten.

In spite of the culture shock, we loved Mexico. We loved the people, the simplicity, and the sincerity. There is a slower pace, and expectations are lower. The Mexican people tend to be more forgiving and understanding--they aren't offended if you are late, assuming that something just must have come up. Overall, they are relationship-oriented, loving, kind, generous and respectful. Material things don't hold any great attachment to them.

Although Juan was still in the care of the orphanage, he was allowed to stay with us for the month of our stay. It was an exciting time for all of us as he joined our family. During that month, Juan started to get to know us better, and we started to get to know him better too. There were three bedrooms in the volunteer house, which worked perfectly with our new arrangements--there was one for Joy and I, one for Chloe and Salome, and one for Juan.

Juan was busy for most of each day with school and his chores in the orphanage, so we mostly saw him at night. We would give him a kiss and put him to bed, just like we had always done for our girls.

Before making the trip to Imuris, Joy and I had prepared ourselves for a very difficult transition, particularly as so many people had thought we were nuts to even consider having a teenager join our family--especially given the fact that we had two younger girls. But the month of September was not difficult at all. Juan was an angel--a beautiful, fun-loving, playful boy, with a great sense of humor. He sang beautiful Christian songs, and was kind and obedient. To us, he seemed like the perfect son.

Juan liked to keep busy all the time and loved to play, spending hours playing with two Matchbox cars. Taking two beetles--we always called them June bugs--he would put one behind each car, and then, as the insects pushed the little cars along, he would see which beetle would win the race.

Unfortunately, the joyous family times we had together that month completely belied the difficulties that lay ahead.

Early in September, we went, as a family, to deliver the adoption papers to the DIF in Navojoa. I had spent a month working on them at home to ensure that I had all the proper international seals, and hoped that everything was correct.

Although the Mexican office had previously told me that there should not be any problems, the US side had admitted that although the adoption would technically be possible, it was practically impossible.

With this conflict of advice, we arrived at the Navojoa office, and gave them the three-inch tall stack of papers. We were told that everything was in order and that the adoption should be done in two months.

"So far, so good," we thought.

Even better, the DIF gave us a document that officially gave us the right to have custody of Juan until the adoption could be completed. After that, we met with Juan's family, and took them all out to eat. Although it was slightly awkward, there was no question that everyone seemed to be happy for Juan.

Over the meal, we told Juan's family of our plan and hope to move to Mexico for two years, in order to serve at the orphanage and complete the adoption of Juan.

Sara was thrilled. Her prayers for her son were finally being answered.

CHAPTER TWENTY-NINE

* * *

Between Two Worlds

* * *

Love is an act of endless forgiveness,
a tender look which becomes a habit.

-Peter Ustinov

"Shouldn't they have called on us by now?" I asked Joy, who merely gave me a "How should I know?" shrug.

I couldn't sit still. I tried, but then I'd be overwhelmed with the urge to get up and walk. So I ended up pacing back and forth in the lobby outside the conference room. I was impatient, but Joy, on the other hand, seemed perfectly at ease.

"I wonder why it's taking so long," I asked myself out loud. Then, remembering the recent meeting, added in complete disgust, "Man, I sure stammered around a lot!"

Joy smiled as if to say that I was being too hard on myself.

The meeting which had led to my nervous pacing was with our church Mission Committee. The brothers had all been very kind, and had asked us to share with them about our experiences in Imuris during September, and about how we felt the Lord was leading us. There were several other questions, but my mind is a blank about most of the interview. One thing I do remember, with painful clarity, is me stammering and struggling to put together my thoughts. Meanwhile, Joy had been calm and collected, quoting scripture, and speaking graciously. I was very glad that Joy had made such a wonderful impression, because I figured the Committee would send her to Mexico for sure--and of course, if that was the case, I would get to go along too.

I hadn't been at all nervous in the lead up to the meeting, and I wasn't even that nervous during it. But something that one of the brothers said to me, immediately before the meeting, threw me completely off balance.

Before the interview, I had prepared a report on our experience in Mexico, as well as a synopsis of what we felt called to do. I was all set and ready to face the committee, until the brother encouraged me to share, for the sake of time, *only* those thoughts that I had *not* already included in my report.

After that bit of advice, I found that every time the committee asked a question, all I could think of to say was information that was already in the report! Whenever I began to say something, I would stop and try to think of a way to say it differently. The brother's request shouldn't have thrown me--but it did. The result was that I stumbled badly in the interview.

For the first time, while waiting for the committee to make its decision, I began to doubt whether they would indeed send us to Mexico. Up until that time, it seemed like almost everyone had doubts, except us. Now it was my turn.

We had become used to people sharing their doubts, and saying things like, "Do you really think that the Mission Committee is going to agree to send you?" This was never meant to be a slam, although I suppose I could have taken it that way. Instead, what they really meant was that our church was ultra-conservative with respect to foreign mission work, and the idea of sending a missionary was still *very* new.

At that time, our church had only one congregation in Mexico, which had been started by a brother who had waited many years before receiving permission to go. Consequently, from a historical perspective, it really was preposterous for us to believe that the Mission Committee would even consider sending an inexperienced couple like us. Nevertheless, we had sensed a recent change with respect to "sending," and were feeling very optimistic. Adding to that optimism was the fact that we were sure that we had been called, and so it only seemed reasonable that the Lord would be leading the committee to that same conclusion.

These were just some of the thoughts that were racing through my mind when the committee finally welcomed us back into the conference room, and shared the good news that they were going to send us to the orphanage in Mexico, according to the plan we had presented.

At last we knew for sure that we would be going, as well as how we would be going, and where we would be going.

With great anticipation, we began making our plans to go full-time starting January 1, 2003--exactly one year to the day since my first trip to Imuris! As well as the excitement of our impending move to Mexico, we were also looking forward to having Juan live with us as our new son.

Once again, many people shared their doubts with us about this decision.

"Think about what you are doing," they would say. "You don't speak the same language. You're from different cultures. He has a troubled past, and is going into his troublesome teenage years. You have two younger girls...." The list of concerns went on, and on, and on.

"You don't know, Juan," we would say. "It will be OK."

We knew that it was going to be difficult at times, but we felt like it was God's will. So, whatever the outcome, we had peace about taking Juan into our home. Also, given how well we had gotten along with him in September, we were cautiously optimistic about the future. But we really didn't know what we were in for.

Although we knew that Juan had a "sad history," we didn't know any of the specifics, or how these dark skeletons from the past would affect our relationship with him.

In my life, I had conquered academics, developed complicated software, and even built a successful business, but a 13-year-old boy was about to present challenges that rivaled all that ... and more. There would be much laughter and tears in the months ahead--but, through it all, there would also be many opportunities to learn and grow.

CHAPTER THIRTY

* * *

Our New Son

* * *

When I was a boy of fourteen, my father was so ignorant
I could hardly stand to have the old man around.
But when I got to twenty-one, I was astonished at how much
he had learned in seven years.

–Mark Twain.

Joy and I had both been very anxious to get back to Mexico and pick up where we had left off in September. As we neared the end of our long journey in January, 2003, I couldn't help but think that crossing the border was a little like going to heaven, in that we had to leave so much behind.

We had rented our house in Francesville to our cousins, who had agreed to let us leave many of our things there. This was necessary, as we were only able to take with us those things that would fit in our minivan. This was such a strong reminder that when we, at last, go home to heaven, we will leave all of our earthly possessions behind.

During our stay in September, Joy and I had fallen in love with the children. Now, as we headed back, we knew that we were returning to so many needs, and we didn't quite know where to start. With as many as 120 children in the orphanage, there was always someone knocking on our door for something or other--sugar, an egg, paper, scissors, tools, photocopies, telephone, the computer, drink, food, the newspaper, medical attention, a ride to town, counseling, glue, toilet paper, flashlight, extension cord ... the list was endless.

Upon arriving at Casa de Elizabeth, Joy and I sat down with the orphanage directors, Manuel and Gaby. They encouraged us to continue the work we had begun in the Bible studies and other types of help, but the thing they most wanted was for us to say bedtime prayers with the children. I took this to heart and tried to say prayers with the boys several nights a week. This became a very special time, as the children liked to ask deep questions about life, which gave me an opportunity to share with them and then pray with them.

For the first six months I went to bed with a headache every night--reminiscent of my time in September. Once again, I attributed this to the stress caused by being forced to learn the language in such a short time. We worked hard at it because we really wanted to be able to communicate with the children and adults at the orphanage. It wasn't all that long before our hard work paid off, and we were all feeling pretty comfortable with our newly acquired language skills. Our girls learned even faster--Salome was fluent in six months, and Chloe in about one year.

We learned a lot of words that were not in any of our books, or even in the dictionary, for that matter. Several examples were bad words, and I made the mistake of using a few of them before I realized. Strangely enough, although I couldn't say a four letter word in English without cringing, I could say a bad word in Spanish without feeling any shame at all.

On top of throwing ourselves headlong into the endless work at the orphanage, we also took on the new challenge of raising a troubled teenager.

Juan was a great blessing in many ways, but as we got to know each other better, the "honeymoon" period started to wear off. Over time, Juan became more difficult, less obedient, and even rebellious.

Anyone who has ever raised a teenager will tell you that a parent needs to be a combination of detective, psychologist, and coach. A bit of mind-reading and ESP doesn't hurt either. The stress of raising even a biological child through adolescence has the power to test the metal of most parents. With Juan, it was even more interesting because we were getting together without the benefit of 13 years of bonding. Added to that was the problem that we were from totally different backgrounds, and had a major language barrier. We also had our two girls, Chloe and Salome, who were both younger than Juan. In retrospect, it seems ridiculous that we even tried such an arrangement--but we always knew that this was part of God's calling for us.

The wide variety of cultural differences was the first thing I noticed when trying to build a relationship with Juan. These differences were as hard on Juan as they were for the rest of us. It took time for us to even recognize some of these differences, and even longer to deal with them. For example, Juan rarely said "please" or "thank you." Although this might seem like a small thing, we were so accustomed to these words being used, that we automatically felt offended if someone didn't use them. It seems quite trivial now, but it pains me to say that it really bothered us that Juan never said these words. But it was something that he soon learned as he became more accustomed to us, and our ways.

In the beginning, there were a multitude of issues that we needed to deal with. In and of themselves, they were all quite minor and insignificant, but when grouped together, they made the initial adjustment more of a challenge. For example, it should come as no surprise that someone who grew up without electricity would never think to turn off the lights. Someone who had never had a clean bathroom--if they ever had a bathroom--is not going to know how to keep a bathroom clean. During that time, whenever we saw a mess in the bathroom, we generally had a pretty good idea who had made it.

One Saturday morning, quite early in our time together, I discovered another, far more troubling, difference....

"Juan! Juan! It's time to get up," I called, trying to wake the sleepy teenager.

"Go away," came the muffled reply.

"It's time to get up. Come on," I insisted.

"It's Saturday. I want to sleep in." Juan protested.

"You *did* sleep in," I pointed out. "It's almost 9AM. Time to get up."

"But why?" the boy asked, before stating what he thought was the obvious reason to stay in bed. "It's Saturday."

"I know it's Saturday," I replied. "I have a list of things for us to do today."

I had been looking forward to working with Juan, and had especially planned some projects that I thought he would enjoy helping me with.

"Saturday is a day of rest," Juan said.

"No," I disagreed. "Saturday is a day of work. Sunday is the day of rest."

Juan did not agree, and was quick to tell me so. "No. Saturday is for rest, and Sunday is for going to church."

We appeared to have a stalemate.

"Juan, I saved these projects just for you, so that we could work together." I was starting to feel frustrated as I sensed that Juan had no desire, whatsoever, to work with me. I was right.

"I don't want to."

"Why not?" I asked, feeling hurt.

"Because I don't like to work."

"Well, you are going to do it--whether you like it or not!" By this stage, I was getting a little angry.

And so it would go ... day after day.

The idea of having a son had been so exciting, and I had so many ideas about what it would be like. I imagined us working together, with Juan interested in learning from me. What I hadn't realized was that this was completely against his nature. He felt as though he had been cheated out of his childhood--never having a chance to play enough--so he wanted to make up for lost time, and because of that, would play whenever he had the opportunity.

Juan always wanted to be busy doing something, like learning soccer, skateboarding, or playing basketball--anything, it seemed, but do something with me. It was as if he knew I loved him, but he didn't want to love me.

Again, it pains me to say it, but I have to admit that the first few months with Juan were a huge disappointment for me. Without question, this was because I had always had an idea in my mind of what it would be like to have a son. I thought a son would look up to me, love me a lot, and want to be with me. With Juan, I believe that he loved us all, but he showed it the least of all to me.

He was more loving with Joy and the girls, and I felt rejected. After all, I was the one who loved him the most. Even though I knew that we weren't adopting Juan for my sake, and I certainly didn't want to be selfish and think only of myself, I soon realized that the only thing I was getting out of our relationship was hurt feelings.

Nevertheless, I did my best to put my feelings aside, because we weren't adopting Juan for me--we were doing it to help him.

One night, as I was saying goodnight to Juan, I shared a little with him about how I was feeling.

"Did you have a good day?" I asked.

"Un-huh."

"Good ... goodnight then. Sleep well," I said with a smile, kissing him on the forehead.

"You too."

Then, before leaving the room, I cheerfully said, "I love you, Juan."

"Good night," he responded.

It was like a blow, but I hesitated to say so. Finally, I said, "Juan, I feel bad asking you this, but do you love me?"

"Yes," he replied after a pause.

"That's nice," I said, before adding, "It's just that you never say it, and so I wonder if you do. I tell you that I love you, but you never respond by saying 'I love you, too,' or anything like that."

We were both silent for a moment.

"Bob, it's just that I grew up different than you." Juan explained. "You are always saying that you love me, and I have never had anyone tell me that until now. It's all very new to me. Just give me time."

It was then that I began to understand that Juan just didn't know how to interact with a father who loved him. After a 13-year absence of this kind of affection in his life, it was hard for him to adjust. He wanted to be a part of our family, but he felt more comfortable obeying Joy than me. This must have been because he naturally felt more affinity for the "mom" figure than the "father" figure, which in the past had been the main source of his suffering. It was a painful experience for me, but my love for him was growing daily. Even so, sometimes it seemed like Juan was becoming more and more distant.

Nevertheless, I forced myself to focus on helping Juan, rather than on my own feelings. I knew that love should be unconditional, and there were times when things went better.

Eventually, Juan began saying, "I love you too," every once in a while, which really warmed our hearts.

Regardless of all the adjustments, I was actually bonding with Juan--and he with me.

CHAPTER THIRTY-ONE

* * *

When Two Worlds Collide

* * *

The most difficult thing in the world
is to know how to do a thing
and to watch someone else doing it wrong,
without commenting.

–T.H. White

The first six months in Mexico were a joyful time of discovering, in a deeper way, the interesting differences between the American and Mexican cultures.

We once took a vehicle to one of the nicer automotive repair shops in town. The work area was nothing more than a dirt floor under a partial roof, with only two walls. There were several cars in the workshop, with parts strung all around them on the ground. But there were no tools to be seen--no work benches, no machines, nothing.

I was wondering how they could possibly take the cars apart without tools, so I started looking around for some clue as to how they managed to do it. There was a motor completely torn down, and a mountain of parts, but still no tools to be found.

There were a half-dozen men standing around talking, their clothes black with grease and their hands, arms, and faces soiled as well. Finally, I saw one of the men dive under the hood of a car and start to work. He reached into his pocket and pulled out a tool. Then I noticed that all the men carried their own tools in their own pockets!

Another time we needed to cut a steel rebar in two. We didn't have any bolt cutters, or hacksaw, or anything that I thought could possibly cut through the hard steel. After realizing we had no tools up to the task, I gave up and said that there was simply no way to do the job. But to my surprise, a young man put a large stone under the rebar, picked up an ax, and in just three strong blows had cut the rebar in two. He smiled at me with satisfaction, and said, "We Mexicans know how to get by with the tools we have."

I had to give him that, but I felt like screaming, "You just ruined a $30 ax!" Instead, I said, "I would have never thought of cutting the rebar like that!

The ax was ruined, but at least he got the job done!

A beautiful, healthy example of the simplicity of the Mexican people is the fact that if someone is not hungry, they don't eat. Quite often, the children at the orphanage would not go and eat when the dinner bell rang. I would ask them, "Aren't you going to go eat?"

They would say, "I'm not hungry."

And they wouldn't go.

One culture shock came from the extensive red tape and paperwork necessary for even the smallest of things, such as getting a drivers license, or opening a checking account. You can spend weeks working on these things, and the whole time it seems as though the officials are constantly looking for a reason to say no.

Perhaps the most striking difference between the two countries was in the matter of equal rights for women. While the US has become a leader in promoting this type of equality, Mexico is still a male-dominated society. Every boy has between four and fourteen girls chasing after him. The girls seem so desperate for attention, probably because they don't receive it at home from their fathers.

Men are not expected to be faithful; they are expected to be unfaithful. This was made very clear when I was visiting an accountant in town. While I was there, he asked me, "So how are your girlfriends?"

I'm married," I responded, thinking I had set things straight.

"So, how are your girlfriends? The professional repeated.

"No ... I'm happily married," I tried to explain.

"Oh, *that's* different!" the man replied.

I certainly don't claim to understand all the reasons why the Mexican society, in general, has such low expectations for its men. But one reason would have to be the lack of good role models. Many fathers are drunks, or completely absent from the family. In the other extreme, mothers tend to dote on their sons, never disciplining them, and treating them like kings instead--doing their laundry and making food for them until they get married, or leave home.

An amazing thing about the Mexican people is their attitude toward delay. One day I was sitting with one of my children in the doctor's waiting room. On the wall, a large sign was prominently displayed, asking that all patients arrive promptly for their appointments.

After reading the sign, I gave myself a pat on the back for arriving early for our 10AM appointment--but when the doctor had not shown up by 11AM, I was getting upset. I couldn't believe that the waiting room was full of people, and this guy was over an hour late--and the kicker was that I was the only one getting impatient! Everyone else had read the sign, but were still smiling, talking, and having a good time.

This attitude is reflected in the Spanish language. We soon learned that there are some words that evidently don't translate with quite the same meaning. We soon discovered that "tomorrow" simply means "not today," and nothing more. So it could mean tomorrow, or it could mean a week later, or even a year--possibly never.

In much the same way, "now" means "anytime," "right now" means "some time soon," and "already" means "right now."

This flexibility with time was especially frustrating when I was ordering materials for work teams. Our church would send groups of volunteers for a week at a time, in order to work on construction projects. It was my job to have all the materials and plans ready to keep everyone busy.

When materials were not going to turn up on time, my challenge was to impress on the hardware store how very important it was for everything to arrive soon. I couldn't have 40 people come 2000 miles to do a job in one week, and have them all standing around because the materials weren't available. But whenever I insisted on a delivery date or time, the Mexicans would look at me as if to say, "Who do you think you are?!"

Being in a hurry is perceived as arrogance. People generally are not in a hurry, and are content to wait. So when we asked for things to be done quickly, it gave the impression that we believed we were more important than everyone else.

All these things were a part of the joy of understanding our differences--the differences that appear when two worlds collide.

Joy and I had to laugh at ourselves one day while visiting some friends near the orphanage. A neighbor saw our car, and asked if we would be willing to take some meat back to the orphanage to store in the cooler there. When we said that we would be glad to, they asked us to back our van into their yard, closer to their little house.

While we were waiting, they opened the hatchback of our minivan. At that instant, Joy and I both had the same thought, and in unison said, "You do think the meat is in plastic, don't you?!"

We looked back over the seats just in time to see them throwing a huge piece of butchered cow into the back of our car, which promptly sank under the weight. Joy and I then watched as a few smaller pieces followed the first. As they did, we could only be thankful that our friends' neighbors had put a piece of cardboard down first. Even so, that didn't keep the blood from getting on the back of the seat, or the sides of the van.

Joy and I still laugh about the looks on our faces when we saw all that unpacked red meat being tossed into our car.

One thing was for certain--we sure weren't living in Francesville anymore!

CHAPTER THIRTY-TWO

* * *

At Home in an Orphanage

* * *

God has given us two hands –
one to receive with and the other to give with.
We are not cisterns made for hoarding;
we are channels made
for sharing.

–Reverend Billy Graham.

It wasn't long before we were feeling at home at the orphanage, and had settled into a routine of sorts. I was teaching four Bible classes and one English class each week, in addition to my other activities and work projects. The days went by fast, and we quickly learned to become more flexible, as our plans were often changed at the last minute.

It is hard to explain the orphanage environment to someone who has never visited Casa de Elizabeth, but try to imagine 35 teenagers, 60 elementary students, and 10 preschoolers, all living together under one roof.

The children faced all of the same challenges that our own children do when growing up, but in addition, they also often suffered from loneliness as a result of missing their relatives. We saw tears on almost a daily basis, and often didn't understand how parents or family members could neglect these beautiful, young people. Joy and I could only listen as they shared their heartrending stories, then offer a shoulder for them to cry on, and a prayer to give them comfort and strength.

One day we went to pick up five children--three brothers and two sisters--who had been abandoned by their mother. They were beautiful children, aged between 5 and 11 years old.

I asked why their mother was giving them up for adoption, because I wanted to believe that it was because she wasn't able to care for them and wanted them to have a better life. I was told that she simply did not want them any more.

For a few days there were a lot of tears, as these little ones learned that they had been put in an orphanage. Even though we wanted, with all our hearts, to comfort these dear little ones, there was very little we could do to take their pain away. So, no matter how small, we made sure that we did whatever we could.

Activities were an important part of life in the orphanage, and I enjoyed taking groups of the boys on hikes, or down to the river to swim. The only difficulty was determining which of the boys to take each time. There was no way that I could possibly supervise 50 boys by myself outside the walls of the orphanage, so each time I had to choose who would go, and who would miss out. Sometimes it seemed like it would have been much easier to not even try, because inevitably there would be some who were very happy with my decision, while the others would be very sad. It was always hard, but I did my best to make it fair so that everyone was able to have a regular turn.

Even so, taking 25 to 30 boys to the river to swim still required a lot of attention and supervision. I was always very glad that the water was only waist deep, and I didn't have to worry too much about any of them drowning. All the same, it was a fulltime job being a one-man attentive audience as they did their little stunts. For the hour that we were there, I would spend virtually the whole time smiling and saying, "Good job!" or "Ata boy!" They all wanted that affirmation, no matter how trivial their feat. So even if it was something as simple as putting their faces in the water, I made sure they knew I was impressed!

Another job I had with the boys was that of pulling teeth. Invariably a boy would come to me with one that he wanted me to pull, and as soon as that happened, a line would start to form. With about 50 boys at the age when their permanent teeth were coming in, there were always a lot of teeth to be pulled. One day I pulled nine teeth, and there were still boys in line, asking for help. Thankfully, a quick check showed that none of their teeth were loose enough-- otherwise I could have been pulling teeth all day!

As for Juan, he would obey me, but I could tell that it was hard for him. Because of the conflict with his step-father in the past, Juan had promised himself that he would never submit to another man. Now submitting to my authority had become an inner struggle for him. Even though he wanted to do what I asked, it was a real battle--especially if obeying meant that he could not do something that he really wanted to do. If I ever started to get upset or raise my voice, he resisted that much more.

During our first six months of living together as a family, we had many ups and downs. There were some mountain highs, such as the time we were on a long road trip. The girls were asleep in the back of the van, and Juan was riding as my copilot. Out of the blue, he said, "I'm going to follow you. I'm going to walk in your footsteps."

He was being as sincere as could be. In that simple statement, he was saying that he wanted to be a Christian who served the Lord, and he wanted to be a good father someday, not like his real father, Antonio.

Juan blessed us continually with his gift of music. He played the guitar with such skill that I completely lost the motivation to play it myself. I couldn't come close to making that instrument sing the way he did. He has been blessed with the gift of a memory that could hear a song and then play it back. Whenever Juan was sad or happy he could be found strumming his guitar, singing and making beautiful music.

During these early months, Juan learned to say, "I love you, Mom," and "I love you, Dad." This meant so much to us, and we knew that he really did love us, but sometimes, during the low times, it was hard to see.

CHAPTER THIRTY-THREE

* * *

Tears

* * *

They that sow in tears
shall reap in joy.

Psalms 126:5

A father that really loved his son would never abandon him--even if the son was bad. I had told Juan that I loved him and had promised him that I wouldn't abandon him, but Juan evidently still had doubts. Having been rejected before, it was very difficult for him to love and to trust again. He wanted to, but he sometimes wondered if he was unlovable. How could he be sure that we wouldn't send him away if one day he really goofed?

He had scars from the past. He knew he wasn't the perfect son he thought we wanted. He feared he would never measure up to our expectations, so why even try. He felt it was only a matter of time before we told him the bad news, "We don't want you either." The only way he would ever know would be to put us to the test.

We had learned to play basketball together, which was a real thrill for me. But then Juan would break my heart by not wanting to play with me, although he wanted to play with everyone else. It was as if he was deliberately trying to break my heart. It was almost as though he was trying to provoke me to anger, to see if I would abandon him like his other fathers had.

Father's Day came and went, and for Juan it was just another day. There was not a card, or even a word from him--nothing. A month later, in July, he treated my birthday in exactly the same way. It appeared that Juan's only concern was his own playing and desires.

I knew better than to allow these things to hurt me, but they still did, and they took their toll. As much as I tried, I couldn't ignore my wounded feelings. I loved Juan as much as if he had been my own flesh-and-blood son, but it didn't appear that he felt the same connection with me. It seemed as if he was deliberately keeping himself, protecting himself from a potential rejection.

When Juan wouldn't obey me, I felt rejected. Juan's inner anger was against his past fathers, not his mother. So naturally it was easier for him to obey Joy than me. I didn't understand this at the time, so when he was more willing to obey Joy than me, I felt like a fool.

I tried to reason with him constantly, in the hope that we might be able to build some sort of father/son relationship--and I was not about to give up. Achieving this goal had become just like every other thing that I had ever completely invested my life into. Failure was not an option. Yet, everything was pointing in that direction.

We weren't the only ones who could see the growing problem. Trusted friends told us, confidentially, that they believed Juan was not good for our family. His quiet rebellion was stressing my relationship with Joy. It was also affecting the girls. Chloe was, quite rightfully, becoming jealous of my time, and wondering if I loved Juan more than her because I spent more time with him trying to solve problems.

As this struggle continued, I found myself often thinking about how our heavenly father has adopted us. His desire is to have a relationship with us, but way too many times we treat Him in the same way that Juan was treating me. We know He loves us and wants to spend time with us, yet we seem to have time for everything else but Him. He wants to help us, but we don't listen to Him. We are so busy with our own lives, that we not only deny him our time and attention, but we turn around and give that time to others instead. We say we love the Lord, but our actions prove otherwise. The parallel between this, and my desire for a father/son relationship with Juan, was amazingly similar.

I was tired and at times wanted to throw in the towel. It was during one of the low times that I found out that Juan had not been honest about an important area. It was no secret that there was a great deal of drug trafficking in the Imuris area. We were close enough to the border that there were staging points and drug activity all over.

Everyone knew who those most involved in the trade were--they didn't hold jobs, and yet drove brand new cars and had expensive toys.

There were various clans with this mafia world. Usually they respected each other's turf, but occasionally there would be news about a murder in the area. The newspapers often carried the grotesque photos of the bloody bodies.

One time, soon after an election, Manuel, the director of the orphanage, told me that I would see two changes. The first was that there would be more checkpoints on the roads heading north for a while. The purpose of these was not to stop all the drug trade, but just that of the competition not in cahoots with the new governing party.

The second change, I found harder to believe. Manuel said that one of the local drug dealers in town would be killed as a sign that there was new leadership in control and he had to be respected.

Sure enough, both occurred. The road blocks went up, and a few days after the election a shot rang out near enough to the orphanage that I heard it.

They said a car drove up to one of the houses bordering the orphanage, a man got out and shot a young, well-known drug dealer dead. No one even bothered to call the police until Manuel made an anonymous call. Everyone was afraid to call--but it didn't matter, because the police didn't come anyway.

Everyone knew what happened and what it meant. The mafia ruled, and there wasn't any policeman willing to die for his $60 a week paycheck.

As a family, we always felt pretty safe, in spite of the lack of the rule of law. We knew, and everyone else knew, that we were there to do a good work. So I felt like as long as we were no threat to anyone involved in the drug trade, we would continue to be fairly safe.

Then one day I was horrified to learn that Jake had gotten involved with people in this illicit trade. He was 14 years old and dabbling in things that he had no business with. Quite frankly, it frightened me because we were outside our own country, and we were more vulnerable. Although I had grown to feel relatively safe in Mexico, there was still a certain uneasiness because we were foreigners. Jake was not only putting himself in danger, but the rest of us as well.

And so about seven months after we had moved fulltime to Mexico, we had reached the point where we didn't think we could keep Juan in our home any longer. But it wasn't just us--Juan was feeling frustrated too. He didn't like rules, and he didn't like being told what to do. He didn't even like having someone watching out for him. It seemed like Juan just wanted was to go back to his mother in Navojoa, where he thought he could do whatever he wanted.

There seemed to be no winning solution, so finally Juan and I sat down on a bench outside of our casita, to talk.

"Juan, I don't know what to say," I began. "I love you, and I don't want to give up. But it seems like we have really, *really* tried, and this just isn't working out."

Almost too eagerly, Juan replied, "No, no, that's fine. I really want to go. I've talked with my mom, and she says I can go to school back there."

I had my doubts that he could, but I didn't say anything. Instead, I asked, "Are you sure?"

"Of course I'm sure," Juan said, dismissing my concern. "How many times have we talked about this? It just doesn't work for me to be here. I am different from you all. You want me to say 'I love you,' and things like that. I don't even know what love is!"

"But there have been times when we got along real well." I wasn't willing to let everything slip away that quickly.

"Yeah ... but look at all the problems we have had too. Look at the problems I have caused in the family. I don't want to cause problems between you and Joy. I'd rather die than do that. I don't care what happens to me."

Anguish pierced my heart as I realized that Juan was feeling the same type of guilt from causing problems with us, that he had felt in his other family.

"Well I care," I responded, without hesitation. "I want what is best for you. Yes, it has been difficult, but anything worthwhile is difficult. Even though it doesn't seem like it, I like to think that you love me."

"I *do* love you. I wouldn't have stayed here this long if I didn't. I just don't know how to show it. I wasn't brought up that way."

"But sometimes you obey really well and are so good--and then other times you do the dumbest things."

"That's why I need to leave," he explained. "I will never be like you want me to be--I just can't do it."

There was a long silence as we both sat on the bench and thought about what had just been said. Eventually I broke the quiet by asking, "Are you really sure, Juan?"

His answer was quick and straight to the point. "Yes."

"Well ... when do you think you would go?" I was thinking that he may want to leave in a couple of weeks, which would be closer to the time when school would be starting again.

Without pausing to think, Juan replied, "Tomorrow."

In an instant, my mind flashed back to the sad-eyed little boy who had looked up at me, as I was leaving after my first visit, and asked, "No tomorrow?"

With the end now in sight, I thought about all the good times we had shared with Juan as a family, and the special moments when he had been tender and said that he loved me. I really believed that he did, and that it was his demons from the past that we were fighting against.

At last, we had reached what appeared to be the time to give up, and I was prepared to do what everyone had been telling us to do for so long. But even at this point, there was something within me that still didn't want to quit. Love never fails. Love suffers long ... but how long? Was it love to let Juan go just because he had given up on himself?

It was then that I was struck with the reality of his leaving, and I began to weep. At first, I tried to hold it back, but the sorrow of both the struggle and the failure was overwhelming. I had given everything I had to give to rescue Juan, and received nothing but pain in return. All my dreams of how it would be to have a son, were finally dashed.

I was so tired of the long talks and arguments, but still so torn. I wanted to quit ... and yet I loved Juan dearly. In fact, we loved all the children we had met at the orphanage. There were so many needs, and I wanted to do something to help them, and give them hope for the future.

As far as I was concerned, investing in the lives of these young people was more important than that huge HP contract and the money we made on it. I believed with all my heart that it would have an eternal dividend. That was the goal, but now with Juan, we were giving up--and I was heartbroken. If I couldn't help Juan, then who could I help? If all the time, love and effort we had invested in him didn't make a difference, then what hope was there of helping anyone else? I felt like our coming to Mexico would be in vain. Words failed me. All I could do was mourn.

"Bob, don't cry. Why are you crying?" Juan's voice was full of concern, but I couldn't respond. I could feel his arms wrapped around me in a firm hug, and although I tried to reciprocate, I had no strength.

"Don't cry, Bob!" I heard his voice break and realized that he was crying too. Over and over again, Juan kept asking me why I was so upset, and telling me not to cry. It was the first time he had ever seen me break down like that.

Finally, I managed to say through my tears, "I don't want you to go." There was conviction in every word. That is all I could think to say.

"OK," he said. "I'm not going."

"You're not? I asked, dumbfounded at the sudden turn of events.

"No, I'm not. How can I, when I know how much you really love me?" Juan said, tears running down his cheeks.

"Juan, I have never really wanted you to leave," I explained. "I just want you to *try* to change."

"OK, I will try," Juan said solemnly, before adding the condition, "just promise me you will never cry again. I cannot stand to see you cry." He sobbed.

After that day, we saw a positive change in Juan. It was as if he finally was learning to trust me and was bonding to us. He showed greater respect, and was much better at obeying. Best of all, almost every day he told us that he loved us. There were joyful times when I would tell him, "You are the best son in the world," and he would say, "You are the best father in the world!"

It seemed that the worst was over, but there were still more chal-lenges ahead. God was really just beginning to work in Juan's heart--and ours.

CHAPTER THIRTY-FOUR

* * *

A Call in the Darkness

* * *

May you live all the days
of your life.

-Jonathan Swift

I t had been a beautiful, sunny afternoon, which had turned into a perfect, warm, summer night

The plaza was packed with youth, ranging from small children to young adults. The sound of children's laughter, and jovial conversations, filled the air, belying the fact that a battle was about to start--a real battle between good and evil; a battle for the hearts and souls of the young people that were present.

Our singing group looked fantastic. We had set up the drum set, microphones, guitars and speakers at one end of the basketball court. Then, as soon as the group leader welcomed everyone to join us, and the musicians strummed the first chords, about a hundred young people surrounded the court.

The talking and horseplay subsided, as all eyes focused on the group of teenagers. This was one of our first events for youth, and we were nervous. These were hardened youth from the rough streets of Bahia Kino, and we really had no idea how they would react to the gospel message being shared by their fellow teens

For a while, Joy and I had been helping our American friend, John, with his "Semillas de Cristo," or "Seeds of Christ," ministry. John was a regular visitor to Casa de Elizabeth, working with adolescents from both the orphanage and the surrounding community. He held meetings to prepare programs for children, and youth evangelism, and I helped where I could--mainly with the music and coordinating events.

Juan had committed his life to Christ, and was excited about participating in Semillas. His singing and guitar playing talents were quickly put to good use in the group. However, as he stood that night to sing and perform with his fellow teens, he felt great fear at the reality of facing so many of his peers, who might ridicule him for his belief in Jesus.

But Juan's emotions were nothing when compared to those of two other members of the group who were actually from Bahia Kino. They were facing cousins, old acquaintances, even parents, who did not share their Christian views. What little religion there was in Bahia Kino was predominately Catholic. Christians were in the minority and were looked down on as being simple-minded.

One of our strongest singers, Elvira, was from Bahia Kino, and we had planned for her to give her testimony that night. But as the group began to sing, they immediately noticed that there was a problem-- Elvira wasn't singing, and without her voice to carry the melody, the song was very weak. The girl was feeling the pressure, and this then distracted the rest of the singers. It was very obvious that Satan was not about to let this group pull off a good show without a fight.

Our talented drummer, Daniel, was a foundational element of the group, and was, like Elvira, also visiting his hometown. When the singers stopped singing, Daniel stopped playing the drums, which left just the guitars--and, before long, they began to fall apart too.

We didn't know what to do. Nothing like this had ever happened before. As the crowd began to whisper, we suddenly understood what was happening. However, even though we realized that it was peer pressure that was affecting the team, we didn't know how to fix the problem in the middle of the show.

Feeling totally helpless, I looked over at John to see if he had any ideas. When I saw his head bowed in prayer, I quickly did the same.

Juan was standing in the second row behind the girls, and the beautiful song they were trying to sing was, "What Would I Have Been":

"Que sería de mí....
What would I have been,
If you wouldn't have found me?
Where would I be today
If you wouldn't have forgiven me?
I would have an emptiness in my heart,
I would be wandering around without direction,
If it wasn't for your grace and your love."

As I prayed for the group, I heard Juan begin to sing loudly and with conviction. He belted out the words in a clear, strong voice,

"Sería como un pájaro herido....
I'd be like a wounded bird
That lay dying on the ground
Like a deer searching
For water in the desert
If it wasn't for your grace and your love."

I stopped praying and looked up. I could see that Juan was singing with all his heart. His eyes were closed, and tears were running down his cheeks. There was a look of passion and determination on his face. My heart was moved.

Slowly the other singers started to join back in, followed closely by the guitars. Daniel never did get started again, but at least the group got through the song.

The rest of the event went without any problems. They performed the dramas, and Elvira did find the grace to share her testimony of how she had found hope and peace in Jesus Christ.

As soon as the group finished, I was compelled to give Juan a hug and tell him how proud I was of him and the whole group.

"I've got something I need to tell you," he said quite seriously, in reply to my encouragement. There was look of urgency on his face.

"OK, I'm all ears."

But Juan hesitated, as if changing his mind. "Not now ... later," he said, then walked away, leaving me with my mouth hanging open.

I sensed that something significant had happened, so I was anxious to hear about it. Later we talked....

"What happened out there, Juan?" I asked quietly.

"I felt so bad to see everyone falling apart because of the peer pressure," he explained. "I felt the presence of the devil, and it felt like he was winning--and there was nothing I could do about it. I started to panic, because I didn't know what to do. But then I started to pray...."

Juan stopped, and I could tell that he was thinking. It was as if he was still trying to sort out what had happened for himself.

"Then what?" I encouraged.

"You're not going to believe this," he warned. "In the midst of all that, I sensed a peace come over me--I don't know how to describe it. And I heard a voice in my head."

Even as he spoke, Juan shook his head in disbelief.

"What did it say?" I prodded.

"He said--just as clear as I am talking to you now--he said, 'Don't worry, Juan. Just follow me. Just do what you can, and I will do the rest!'"

"Wow!" I exclaimed with excitement. "That's incredible, Juan! You should tell the others."

I wanted to tell the whole world, but thought the team should know first. So it came as a surprise when Juan shook his head and said, "No, I don't want to."

"Why not?" I asked, amazed that he wouldn't want to share this with anyone else.

"No, don't tell anybody," he said, quite emphatically.

"But Juan, this is a tremendous calling. It's incredible! It's clear that God is calling you, isn't it?"

Juan was quiet.

"Can't I even tell Joy?" I asked, but he shook his head.

"I'll tell her when I'm ready. Don't say a word to anybody ... understand?"

"OK, fine," I consented, although with great difficulty.

I didn't really understand, but apparently Juan did not feel ready ... or perhaps even worthy to have received such a call. Often times he had expressed his fear of being a Christian, because he was afraid that one day he would fall and people would call him a hypocrite.

Even so, for whatever reason, the calling sobered Juan, and he kept it to himself.

Like any teenager, Juan had the tendency to keep things inside. One time when he returned from visiting Navojoa, I noticed that he was fairly subdued. When I asked him why, he said he had met his biological father for the first time. I asked him about it, but Juan said they had only spoken a few words.

Apparently, the first thing Antonio had asked was, "Why did your mother give you away?"

Juan told him that his mother had not given him away, but that he had chosen to go.

It had to have been a very traumatic experience for him. I was glad he was able to share it with me. He had told me before that if he every met his real father he was going to kill him. I had obviously tried to talk him out of that. Hopefully, in the process of meeting the man, he was beginning to sort these feelings out. I always tried to channel the feelings in a positive direction as I would counsel Juan how to someday be a good father and take care of his children.

CHAPTER THIRTY-FIVE

* * *

The Rough Road to Heartache

* * *

Life is an exciting business and most exciting
when it is lived for others.

–Elie Wiesel

The car was, without a doubt, in the worst shape that I had ever seen any vehicle that could still actually propel itself down the road under its own power! We put in a few gallons of gas, and two quarts of oil, which effectively doubled the car's value!

Juan and I had taken the bus to Navojoa, once again, to check on his adoption--which didn't appear to be progressing. While there, we decided to make the most of our trip by checking on some dear children we had known at the orphanage, who had since returned to Navojoa to be with their single mother.

I wanted to take the public transit bus, but Juan's stepfather, Nataniel, insisted that we take his "new" car. The transit bus was an adventure in itself, because of the maniac way the drivers careen over bumps and hills, and around tight corners. Although I often felt like I was putting my life on the line to get on one of those buses, it still looked like a far more reliable way to get across town than the alternative--Nataniel's car.

It was an old, windowless, Dodge Omni, and although it did have doors, the latches didn't work. There was not a bit of paint on the exterior, and there wasn't really any interior, or dash. It was just metal and motor--and not much else.

Nataniel insisted that we "drive." All I had to do was buy the gas. I knew his kind offer was just a way for him to get me to buy gas. He said he only had enough to get to the gas station, and he was right. He pulled out a two-liter Coke bottle, that was about a third full, and poured the foamy, orange, fluid into the tank.

We worked for 15 minutes to get the engine started, and another 10 to just get the wreck into the street.

The motor was popping and backfiring so badly that it hardly had enough horsepower to move the car. But there we went, banging and clanking down the street. Nataniel and Juan were both smiling whenever the car was running, but a little more sober when it died. On the other hand, I was mortified. However, once we had made it past the first few motor deaths and resurrections, I found that I, too, was starting to smile when it was running.

What a sight we must have been!

Finally we pulled into the shiny, new Pemex gas station, just as the car's motor died in one final poof of white smoke. I gave Nataniel 100 pesos, and he spent it all on gas and two quarts of oil.

I didn't think that two quarts would be enough, but we never found out because we couldn't get the thing started again after putting the gas in. After a while, we gave up and pushed the car out of the station, parking the heap along the street. Various friends stopped by, all with different advice about what was wrong with the car. They all seemed to have the ability to diagnose the problem simply by looking at it.

In the end, we hitched a ride in the back of a pickup, and eventually arrived to see the three boys that had been with us in Imuris.

When we arrived, I saw straight away that the children were all looking at pornographic magazines--small booklets with the raunchiest filth imaginable. The oldest boy at least appeared to have a sense of shame, and quickly hid his book. The younger two didn't act like there was anything at all unusual or wrong about looking at the things that they were. Obviously their mother knew--in fact, it was quite possible that she had been the one to buy the magazines for them.

It was hard for me to see these dear, beautiful children living in such conditions. Abject poverty, no electricity or water, very little food, shelter or clothing--and yet, someone had paid good money to buy them pornography.

None of the boys would say much to us. One of them hid and would not come out again while we were there.

My heart was sick as we said goodbye and left.

CHAPTER THIRTY-SIX

* * *

For Everything, There is a Season

* * *

Before I got married I had six theories
about bringing up children;
now I have six children,
and no theories.

–John Wilmot, Earl of Rochester

By September of 2003, Joy and I had come to the conclusion that we wouldn't be able to stay at Casa de Elizabeth in Imuris long term. It was a heartrending realization because we dearly loved the children there. There was so much that we wanted to do to help them, especially the youth. We could see so much potential, but it just wasn't being developed.

The plan for the teenagers was for them to apply themselves and work hard in school--but there was no plan for them after they graduated. I looked into what had happened to the teens that had graduated from school. Sadly, what I discovered was very discouraging.

Many never finished school, and those who did rarely completed a degree. The few who went on to college were often unable to find work once they had completed their course.

The problem was the school structure, which was basically one big, social gathering. The students do learn to read and do some math, but outside of that, the only thing they learn really well is reproduction.

Comprehensive sex education begins in elementary school, and by junior high there is an enormous amount of time spent on the subject. Students have to develop clay models of the genitals and also give individual presentations in front of all their peers, where they explain, in detail, the function of the reproductive organs.

The only thing lacking was a "lab" where they could actually practice firsthand. Apparently some pupils did, all the same, as there was very little supervision. Students would regularly leave school during the day, to gather in nearby houses until they chose to return to school later.

I was appalled when I heard that students were leaving school in this way, and doing who-knows-what! However, when I asked about it at school, nobody seemed too concerned. Such was the general attitude.

Added to this was the fact that there always seemed to be an excuse for a "fiesta" or party. These celebrations were taken very seriously, and school would often be called off on the day, so that all the students would have time to bathe and get ready. Quite literally, weeks were spent celebrating various holidays, which goes a long way to explaining why most students were not prepared to hold decent jobs upon graduation.

Although Joy and I had an obvious concern for Juan, we also had a burden for all the teenagers who were being exposed to this sort of school environment, and were not being properly prepared for the real world.

In an attempt to combat this deficiency, we tried to start classes and projects within the orphanage, but were unable to effect much change. Although we sincerely tried, the environment was such that these initiatives soon fell by the wayside. When it is a day-to-day struggle just to have enough food, clothing, and water, such things as educational programs end up taking a back seat. Only the bare necessities survived.

Our church was disposed to offer extra financial help, but wanted greater accountability if they were going to give more money. Unfortunately, the leadership at the orphanage did not consent. Even though they always appreciated the help, the orphanage was not willing to yield any control, or allow for the level of accountability that the donors required. That being the case, the church could not provide the help that we could see was really so desperately needed.

I struggled a long time with wanting to help more, but the director basically made it clear that they didn't need our help in this way. He brushed it off, saying, "A Mexican only needs a tree for shade." I didn't understand why they would turn down help. Then they explained why.

The administration wanted to be completely independent because, in the past, the orphanage had been supported by a single church,. This made them very dependant on that one source of funding. Then when there was a difference of opinion, the church suddenly pulled out, leaving the orphanage without any financial support. They had survived without water, gas or electric for several months. Neighbors brought in food for the children. Soon new sponsors came when they heard of the need.

Because of this, the administration decided they would never again let themselves become overly dependant on any one outside organization again. They had developed a strong spirit of independence and believed that once a dollar was donated, it was theirs, and they could use it wherever they had the greatest need.

After a few months of seeing great needs go unmet, a feeling of futility began to take hold. We wanted, so much, to help these young people, but were slowly coming to the realization that this would not be possible if we stayed at Casa de Elizabeth. To provide the help that we were longing to do, we would need to have more flexibility and control over the program. So, with heavy hearts, we began to look at other options.

We didn't want to leave CE, but we knew we had to. In retrospect, we see this as the hand of the Lord, because if we would have been content with everything at CE, we would have never forced ourselves to step out and start a new orphanage.

It was time to start looking for other projects for World Relief, and so, from that time, we began pursuing other opportunities in earnest. We thought of building a Christian school, or possibly another orphanage, but really didn't know exactly what the Lord had in store. All that mattered was that there was a great need to provide direction, training and hope to so many beautiful, young, potential-laden people--and we wanted to be used by God to do just that.

CHAPTER THIRTY-SEVEN

* * *

Another Door Opens

* * *

When it comes to giving,
some people stop at nothing.

-Sheetz

O nce they were aware of our plans to move away from Casa de Elizabeth, the orphanage directors told us of a property that was for sale in Magdalena. Initially, I wasn't interested, because Magdalena sounded like a long way away from our home at CE. So it was with reluctance that I eventually went to see the property with fellow World Relief worker, Jerry.

As soon as I saw the land, it was love at first sight.

Jerry had been involved with the orphanage at Imuris for many years and had a tremendous heart for the work. He had been incredibly faithful in coming down to visit, and always came bearing apple pies from McDonalds for the girls. Then he would take the rest of us out for a meal. Now, as we stood together on the property in Magdalena, I could see the possibilities written all over Jerry's face.

We both liked the way the property was situated near the river, with its grass and green trees. Here, in the middle of the desert, was this cool valley, surrounded by beautiful mountains and tall saguaro cactus. As an added bonus, there was an existing building on the land, which we thought would be the perfect site for an orphanage and Christian school.

Faced with such a perfect opportunity, Jerry and I talked about the price we would be willing to pay, and agreed that it would probably be between $300,000 and $400,000.

Jerry was ready to buy it on the spot. He had been waiting for an opportunity like this for so long, and he just had a sense that this was right. Adding to this belief was the fact that Joy and I were feeling called to start a new work of this type.

Even so, as ideal as it all seemed, we decided to seriously pray about what God would have us do.

During that time of waiting for God's direction, we shared the idea with a few other people--another missionary from Mexico and the leadership of our church. They were all very positive, but we knew that it would take some time for the church to get the approval to buy the Magdalena property. In the meantime, Jerry and I were worried that someone else might purchase it--in fact, Jerry was even more anxious than me!

Then one day, not long after we had first seen the property, Jerry called from Phoenix. As we talked about our hopes for the land, I said, "I guess I'm not worried all that much about someone else buying it. If it's God's will that we get the property, then it will still be for sale when we are ready for it."

Although Jerry agreed with the truth of what I had said, he added, "But if we are pretty sure that we are interested, and the price is right, then why should we wait?"

"Well," I replied, somewhat cautiously, "I believe God is leading us to buy the property, and that's exciting. Joy and I have always thought we would stay down here for more than two years. So if we do this project, we definitely would stay on."

"Bob, you and Joy are a big part of this," Jerry encouraged. "You need to take the leadership and make it happen."

"I'm just not sure about the timing," I admitted. "Do we go ahead and buy it now, or do we wait until the church approves the project?"

"Bob, it will take six months to get approval."

"At least," I said, acknowledging the reality of what he had said.

"In the meantime, this opportunity could slip away because we've delayed."

In my heart, I felt he was right, so finally said, "I agree."

"So, you agree we should go ahead?"

"Yes, I do ... it's just that I am nervous about making this commitment with your money."

Jerry quickly brushed my concern away. "I'm not worried about that. Worst case scenario--we never use the property. If that happens, I can always resell it."

It made sense. "Well then, I guess so. Like I said, it is your money that's at stake."

"Bob, the truth is that I feel so strongly about this, I would do it with or without you!" he confessed.

Laughing out loud, I made my commitment. "Well, if you put it that way, count me in!"

So we made plans for Jerry to buy the property, and it was purchased in November of 2003. We began work on renovations immediately, and then as soon as the house was livable, Joy--who was gravely ill with Hepatitis at the time--and I moved to Magdalena. By then it was April 2004.

Renovation work continued throughout that year, with remodeling of the office, dormitories, and kitchen. The first children arrived in February, 2005.

Since then, we've had every kind of joy and sorrow imaginable--things like lice and scabies, runaways and fights, heartaches and headaches. But through it all, the Lord has been faithful. Through Him, so many have come to lend a hand ... so many have blessed us with their love and prayers.

In 2005, we had approximately 700 visitors/volunteers come to Magdalena. As of February, 2006, there are about 20 children in the orphanage, and this new work has been a great blessing to our church fellowship, as well as to the children and families we serve. It is the fulfillment of a dream--an answer to God's call. We praise Him for the opportunity to be a part of this work, and give Him all the glory.

CHAPTER THIRTY-EIGHT

* * *

"You saved at least one"

* * *

How selfhood begins with a walking away,
And love is proved in the letting go.

–C. Day-Lewis

While the start of 2006 was a time of great rejoicing as we walked further into the open door that was the orphanage at Magdalena. Sadly, it was also time for another door to close....

I was wearing my sunglasses, but not because it was bright outside. I was wearing them to hide the tears in my eyes. Having always been tenderhearted, there are times when I don't want to cry, but have no control over this emotional response. Usually, I can avoid it by making a conscious decision not to think about whatever it is that's making me sad.

On this particular day, it was hard to avoid thinking about driving Juan to the bus station, because that was exactly what I was doing.

We were both silent in the car. My heart was aching, and I was fighting to hold back the tears, because I knew how much Juan disliked it when I cried. Whenever I cried, it made him cry too.

Every parent has to face the day when their child leaves home. We all hope that it will be a joyous occasion, but at best, it is usually difficult. I'm sure that we would all like it to be with a lot of confidence that we have done everything we could to prepare the child for this big step. But I suspect that most of us are left with the nagging doubt that maybe we could have done more. While hoping that our children are ready, we secretly wonder if they are.

I wish I could say that Juan's departure was a happy one--but it was not. We did feel like we had done everything that we could, and yet, we always felt so inadequate. I know we made many mistakes with him, but we had done our best.

As we drove, I wondered why I was suffering so much. It didn't seem fair. Juan seemed excited to be leaving, but I had a heavy heart. I didn't think he was leaving for the right reasons. I didn't think he was ready for this. I knew I wasn't.

Juan was heading back to Navojoa, the place of his birth, where his mother would dote on him, and not ask him to do anything. I knew that he was looking forward to having more liberty, and not having anyone telling him what he could or couldn't do. But it was more than just the desire for more freedom. I saw the excitement of the unknown in his eyes, and the desire to be an independent man, to begin to make a way for himself in the world.

At 17, Juan was no longer the little boy we found in the orphanage. He had not been the perfect son, but he had learned so much. Now he spoke English fluently and knew there were people who really loved him. Even more importantly, he knew God loved him.

Living with us in the "goldfish bowl" world of the orphanage had not been easy for Juan. The new orphanage in Magdalena was a popular spot and it seemed like our family was under constant scrutiny. We had experienced many ups and downs together. We felt like we were on an emotional roller-coaster at times. But through it all, we had loved Juan as one of our own and wanted the very best for him.

"Aren't you going to come in with me?"

We had arrived at the bus station, and Juan's question brought me back from my thoughts.

"I can't," I said, wiping my eyes.

"Why are you like that?" he asked, seeing my tears.

I shrugged.

"Just think of it as if I'm going away for a two week visit," Juan reasoned.

"You probably will want to come back in two weeks, but you won't be able to save up the money to buy a bus ticket."

"Well ... even so, I've got to go," he said thoughtfully.

Then, reaching over to give me a hug, he said, "I love you Dad."

"I love you too, Son."

"Bye," he said, his voice cracking with emotion.

Juan got out of the car, fighting tears as he went--and then he was gone.

* * *

Just like the rest of us, Juan is still learning how to surrender. God certainly has not given up on him, and neither have we. Our faith is that one day he will completely surrender his heart and life to the Lord, that the call on His life will be answered, and God will use him in a powerful way.

Please join us in that prayer--not only for Juan, but for all the struggling youth in this world, who suffer because of the sins of their forefathers, who are so deserving of more love and care.

One day I confided in Juan that I sometimes fear I will be a failure as a missionary. "Maybe no one will become converted," I said.

Juan smiled wryly and encouraged, "Well you've saved at least one!"

"Who?" I asked dumbfounded.

"Me!" He replied and we both laughed.

"Yes! That's it!" I said, "And you will go on to save a thousand!"

Joy and I thank God for the privilege of being able to have this young man as part of our family. We have learned so much from our experiences with Juan. Just as we had known in the beginning, we still feel that this was part of God's plan. We believe this schooling was God's way to help prepare us for our future work in Mexico.

We never were able to finish the adoption, which is quite a long story. However, suffice it to say that although adoption in Mexico is *technically* straightforward and legal, it is *practically* impossible to accomplish. So even though Juan never legally became our son, in our hearts he will always hold that place.

Just as I have discovered so many other times in my life, I finally realized that I had to surrender Juan as well. With that came the understanding that I can't change him, or anyone else. I know that he knows the truth, and that God will keep calling him. I can't heal his past, or that of any other child. Ultimately, it is God who heals and converts hearts.

We plant, another waters, but God grants the increase. So let's be busy planting and watering!

* * *

Looking back over the first 37 years of my life, I've had to surrender success, materialism, finances, marriage, country, home, children, pride, comfort, security and reputation. I haven't done any of it gracefully--and I still find myself wanting to pick these things up again and again. But hopefully, by God's grace, I am beginning to learn what to surrender, and what to hold onto.

What we never want to surrender, though the way may sometimes be difficult, is our calling. You and I have a God-given purpose the He has created us to fulfill. Don't be discouraged by your imperfections or lack of qualifications. The Bible is full of examples where God uses the most unworthy people. And don't be dismayed by naysayers, or those that will oppose you--yes, you will have opposition.

Pour yourself out and let God fill you. Surrender everything that holds you back, but never what God has called you to do. For it is in answering that call that we have found God's greatest joy and fulfillment.

May it be for you also.

* * *

Oh, to be nothing, nothing,
Only to lie at His feet,
A broken and emptied vessel,
For the Master's use made meet.
Emptied that He might fill me
As forth to His service I go;
Broken, that so unhindered,
His life through me might show.
Oh, to be nothing, nothing,

262

Painful the humbling may be,
Yet low in the dust I'd lay me
That the world might my Savior see.
Rather be nothing, nothing,
To Him let our voices be raised,
He is the Fountain of blessing,
He only is meet to be praised.
Georgiana M. Taylor, 1869

* * *

Postscript ....

‿❦‿

Although the sale of AdaptaSoft didn't turn out to be the financial support we had planned on, God is faithful and has provided everything we have needed. We are happy to report that the company appears to be doing well. They have built a service business around CyberPay, the payroll product that we had developed.

It thrills us to see that they have about 15 fulltime employees in Francesville. It is not yet the 50 we envisioned, but the company has come a long way and is a great blessing to the community, its employees and its customers.

Juan has a good job at a Pemex gas station attending pumps. He is working hard and making good tips from the American travelers with whom he speaks English. He still loves "Mom and Dad" and tells us so often.

Chloe and Salome are finishing up their homeschooling for the year and looking forward to summer vacation. They enjoy their many friends here at the orphanage in Magdalena. They also have many Mexican friends at the Casa Elizabeth orphanage in Imuris, where we still visit.

Joy and I feel that God is leading us to move on from the orphanage we helped start here in Magdalena. Just as it was agonizing to leave the dear children in Imuris, it will be even more so with those that we cared for here. But God has a plan, something else for us to do, and we trust in Him to guide us in the next step. To find out what the "next step" is, go to www.bobjoyhuber.org.

A sincere "thank you" to all of you for all your love, prayers and support!

Printed in the United States
57832LVS00006B/112-255

9 781600 344756

Printed in the United States
57832LVS00006B/112-255

9 781600 344756